THE BIG QUESTIONS BOOK
OF SEX AND CONSENT

ALSO BY DONNA FREITAS

Adult Nonfiction

Sex and the Soul: Juggling Sexuality, Spirituality, Romance,
and Religion on America's College Campuses
The Happiness Effect: How Social Media is Driving a
Generation to Appear Perfect at Any Cost
Consent on Campus: A Manifesto
Consent: A Memoir of Unwanted Attention

Young Adult Fiction

The Possibilities of Sainthood
This Gorgeous Game
The Survival Kit
Unplugged
The Healer

Middle Grade Fiction

Gold Medal Summer
Gold Medal Winter

LEVINE QUERIDO

MONTCLAIR • AMSTERDAM • NEW YORK

THE BIG QUESTIONS BOOK OF

SEX AND CONSENT

BY DONNA FREITAS

This is an Arthur A. Levine book
Published by Levine Querido

www.levinequerido.com · info@levinequerido.com

Levine Querido is distributed by Chronicle Books LLC

Library of Congress Control Number: 2019956998

ISBN 978-1-64614-018-3

Printed and bound in Hong Kong

Published September 2020

First Printing

This book is written in appreciation of the thousands of college students from all over the United States who have spoken to me over the last fifteen years about about sex, love, consent, and everything in between, and who have talked wistfully of all the things they wish someone had told them back when they were twelve. I hope that I did justice to your younger selves.

Contents

PART TWO
Other Things to Consider in Our Effort to Build That Sexually Liberated Utopia
(And That Are Really Important to CONSENT)

PART THREE
Consent

AUTHOR'S NOTE

I have done my best to be sensitive, open, and inclusive of everyone in this book, but—given the fluidity of our discussions and language about identity and diversity—it is inevitable that I may have used language or phrases that will be problematic to some people or may inadvertently make certain readers feel left out. For this, I am sorry, and I ask for your generosity and forgiveness. I also use language and discuss topics that may be offensive to some; I believe that to confront offensive stereotypes and language we must identify the offending material in order to analyze, transform, and rewrite it. My intent is not to harm. My heartfelt hope is to include all readers and to empower all of us in a way that is honest, open, and unflinching. To confront sexual oppression and systemic sexual violence we cannot shy away from the worst of our culture—it is only in facing it that we can change it for the better.

INTRODUCTION

Hello, Hello! Nice to Meet You!

This Is YOUR Safe Space

This Stuff Makes Us Feel Vulnerable

The first time I ever wrote a kissing scene in a novel I was mortified!

I dreaded reaching the moment in the book when I was going to have to figure out how to do it. I read and reread kissing scenes from other novels, hoping for advice, instruction, insight. But every time I thought about having to write one myself, my cheeks flushed bright red and I wanted to cover my face with my hands.

Who, exactly, was I hiding from? And why?

Well, for one, I was a new writer, so I worried I would write a terrible kissing scene. And then, writing a kissing scene made me feel so vulnerable. It felt like a big confession. Like, there I was, admitting my deepest, most secret desires about how two

3

people should kiss or how I had always wished someone would kiss me. The task seemed to involve baring my soul.

When the time arrived for me to write that scene, my heart sped, my palms grew sweaty, my cheeks burned.

I wanted to hide behind a pillow.

I wanted to cover myself with a mountain of pillows!

I actually picked up my laptop and moved to a different spot in my apartment, to the back wall of the living room, in a corner. I actually *turned toward the wall* while I typed.

You know how when you're a little kid and you think if you hide under the covers or face away from someone, then no one can see you? That was pretty much what was going through my head at the time.

But I got through it. Everything turned out fine!

After a while, writing kissing scenes became fun. Though it's also true that writing them will always make me feel vulnerable. It's tough stuff, but it's also good stuff. We learn a lot about ourselves when we do things like this, even though it can be difficult. Vulnerability is part of who we are, and anything to do with desire, romance, and sexual intimacy can draw out that part of us. We need to acknowledge and embrace our vulnerability if we are going to have challenging, important conversations about sex and consent.

✳

In my line of work, which involves talking to college students about sex and consent, people talk a lot about "safe spaces."

The term "safe space" refers to a circumstance or situation where people feel comfortable opening up about a topic, usually a difficult one. Safe spaces are nonthreatening spaces where someone can think through and discuss all the complexities of an issue.

But . . .

I want to say a little more about comfort—specifically discomfort.

There is a *big* difference between feeling nervous and uncomfortable about an unfamiliar topic or an awkward subject, and feeling *threatened*. An unsafe space is a threatening space. A space where you believe someone may intentionally hurt you, or one where someone or something that has already hurt you is present and you do not trust it or them.

But even *within safe spaces* we may feel like we want to crawl under a desk because things get awkward. And sometimes we just may have to crawl under the desk and listen from there. Kind of like how I moved to a different part of my apartment and faced the wall in order to write that kissing scene.

Some of the stuff in this book is going to make you uncomfortable. Squeamish. Confused. Maybe even embarrassed. Maybe you feel that way already. Maybe the moment you saw the title of this book, you rolled your eyes and wanted to throw it out the window. Maybe someone in your family "casually left it" on a coffee table or in the bathroom or even placed it on your bed so you'd "casually find it" when wandering around your house or apartment. Maybe someone gave it to you as a gift and all you wanted to do was return it to the store.

Discomfort, feeling weird and awkward, though, is not a big enough reason to avoid these issues. Sex, consent, and all that goes with it *can* make us uncomfortable because:

* we don't know how we feel about it;

* it's confusing;

* maybe we're inexperienced;

* it makes us feel vulnerable;

* and it's a complex aspect of our humanity.

But just as knowledge is power and understanding empowers us, a *lack* of knowledge and understanding can be *really* disempowering, especially with this subject.

This kind of discomfort is part of life—you can't run from it. You have to learn to live with this kind of discomfort. You've got to push through it because this is one of the most important topics you'll ever think about during your life as a teenager and young adult.

Give yourself time. Thinking and talking about this will get less weird and less awkward the more you do it. As you move through this book, put a pillow over your face if you need to once in a while. Cover yourself in a mountain of pillows if need be.

But you owe it to yourself to stick this out.

You definitely owe it to all your future partners, too.

And Speaking of Partners:
Who Are Your Conversation Partners Here?

I am not your mother. Or your father.

Obviously.

But I know it's likely that whoever is raising you will want to talk about the stuff we're discussing because they love you and worry about you, and like me, they know that these are some of the most important conversations you'll ever have. I also know you probably dread the idea of having those discussions. Almost everybody feels that way. I certainly did. People who don't are rare. It's difficult—sometimes even mortifying—to talk to your parents about these things. It can be strange and weird and awkward. You might even feel allergic to the possibility.

But here is the thing:

If not your parents or grandparents or whoever is raising you, it has to be *someone.* You need people you can talk to—people who are not your peers and friends. Peers and friends are important, too, but you also need adults. We are going to work on helping you think of which adults those might be.

Because you are going to have *lots* of questions—you likely do already.

And I've got good news!

Not all conversations about sex and consent actually require you to talk directly about sex and consent. You'll see as you move through this book that a lot of the questions here are big picture inquiries about identity and even friendship. These may be the places where Mom and Dad are great conversation partners for you.

But for the times when the issues get more direct, when you start to dread the thought of talking to Mom and Dad and Grandma and Tía Sonia about your questions and the reflections I ask you to think about at the end of each chapter (Don't worry! They're fun, I swear!), your job is to find someone else with whom you don't dread a conversation. This may seem daunting—and you don't have to do it right away (phew)—but eventually you'll feel ready. And when you are, this book is here to help!

If there's one thing I've learned from your older peers who are at college, it's how alone they feel when it comes to talking about sex and consent.

You don't have to be alone in this. You shouldn't be.

I don't want you to be.

It will be worth the effort in the long run to be brave and find a few someones you can talk to. Part of creating safe spaces for dialogue about sex and consent involves figuring out who you'd like to share that space with. And everyone is welcome to bring all the pillows they need for support.

Your Very Own List of People to Talk To:

We'll make these first reflection questions super easy, since it's the first.

1. Think of three people in your life with whom you feel like you maybe, could possibly, if you absolutely *had* to, have a conversation about sex. (And you have to come up with three.) Here's the catch: they have to be older than you, ideally people you'd put in the category "adults." Don't overthink it—use your instincts. Just write down those names as they come to you.

2. Now think about *why* those adults. What makes them seem like appealing conversation partners for this subject? Or just in general? Reflect a bit on why they seem like good people to talk to.

3. Last thing: decide on three *friends* you think you could talk to about this stuff. (I'm guessing this list will be easier.) And do the same as above—think about why these three friends, specifically.

I want you to have these six names handy as you consider the topics in this book. This is how you will know you are *never* alone in this. There are people in your life—both adults and your peers—with whom you can share your thoughts and feelings, and maybe even ask a few questions. I always, *always* want you to know who your conversation partners are so if you are ever feeling alone and isolated, you can call up those names and remember that you are *not* alone, and why you are not.

How This Book Works

What This Book Strives For: A Sexually Liberated UTOPIA!!!

(Yeah, yeah. I see you rolling your eyes. Get that cynicism out of your system now, because, like, I'm totally serious about this! Why not aim high?)

So, what is a utopia anyway?

Well, it's kind of the opposite of a *dys*topia, which you're probably already familiar with, because I bet you've read or watched Suzanne Collins's *The Hunger Games*, where children are selected (against their will) to participate in an obsessively watched reality TV–like situation where they fight to the death. Yup. That's about as dystopian as it gets.

With respect to sex and consent and the world we're actually living in? Sometimes I do feel like things are rather dystopian. Instead of doing all that it takes to fight against systemic sexual violence and gender and sex discrimination and shaming, we offer Band-Aids and allow the status quo (how things are now and have always been) to persist. Rather than offering sex education in a way where people like you, the reader, grow up to be empowered and excited about sex and all that goes with it, our culture teaches you to fear sex and gives you only the most negative possible news about what happens if you have it.

But in this book?

We are going to do our best to imagine a very different world. We are going to open our hearts and minds and dream of the best possible circumstances that we humans can envision when it comes to sex and consent. Let's dream a little right now to get ourselves started.

What might a *sexually liberated utopia* look like?

* It's a world that does not know violence, where the notion of using sex as a weapon, as a means to control or have power over, or as a tool of misogynistic intent does not exist.

* It's a world where consent—respect for it, the understanding that it is an essential foundation and ingredient of any sexual intimacy—is not only a priority but a given.

* It's a world that prioritizes and values ethics—sexual and relational ethics.

* It's a world that understands the essential relationship between sexual ethics and consent, and therefore sexual ethics and *all sexual intimacy*.

* It's a world that is inclusive of everyone—that is respectful and inclusive of diversity in every way, including sexual diversity, gender diversity, racial diversity, and religious diversity. We are respectful of differences of all kinds; we consider and understand intersectionality (when social categories like Latinx and bisexual overlap) and the additional challenges that intersectional identities pose for us in our country and our communities. For example: being gay *and* being Latinx, being Black *and* being a woman, being disabled *and* Asian *and* a woman, being Muslim and a lesbian.

* It's a world where sexual diversity is understood as referring to far more than sexual identity and orientation. It understands that there is no one, single, true path for sex—when you have it, where you have it, who you have it with. It respects that not everyone follows the same timeline, for first-time sex or any-time sex. It makes room for both the nonreligious and the religious, and different visions of sexuality.

* It's a world where sex education and sexual violence prevention education looks very different from how it does now. Our methods for education involve posing big, open, complex questions and helping children and young adults build the foundation and framework they'll need to make their way through the many diverse sexual and romantic situations they will encounter in life.

* It's a world where being a critical thinker—about our-selves, about sex, consent, romance, and love—is a goal for all of us, and a priority for all children and young adults. It's a *thoughtful* world and a *thought-filled* world.

* It's a world that respects and celebrates embodiment and all bodies. A world that does not judge or value certain bodies over others and that recognizes and respects the vulnerability of all bodies, regardless of race, ethnicity, gender, sexual orientation, economic status, educational background, and any other par-ticularity that might contribute to the *devaluing* of a particular body.

* It's a world where we do not feel shame about who we are, about our particular desires, about our yearning to love and be loved, about the ways that we are vulnerable.

* It's a world where sex and consent are free from fear and where we do not promote fear around these topics. It's a world that encourages connection, rela-tionship, and care.

* It's a world where sincerity, openheartedness, and enthusiasm are celebrated, affirmed, and encouraged.

* It's a world that values play, playfulness, and fun in relation to sex and sexual intimacy, a world that celebrates pleasure and the giving of pleasure, the joys of flirtation, the excitement of romance and sex, of

being romanced by someone, and the fact that sex is a wonderful aspect of our humanity.

The world I describe is one of great complexity, and in its complexity there is beauty. It is a world where such complexity is celebrated, acknowledged, and respected; where we accept the fact that sex, sexual identity, and gender identity are multifaceted aspects of our humanity; where consent is just as layered; and where the answer to this complexity is *not* to distill these things into easy answers and quick fixes.

This book strives to prepare you, the reader, to be a person who can make that utopia less of a theory and more of a reality. It aims to give you the tools to help create this world—to figure out what creating it might involve. This book intends to ask enough of the Big, Relevant Questions that can help us—all of us—get a little closer to the utopian world existing not just in our imaginations or our dreams, but in reality.

What This Book Is NOT: A How-To About Sex and Consent

I know that in school when you learn about sex, they likely teach you the "how-tos" and the "don'ts" of sex—how your body works, the physicalities of sex, how not to get pregnant, how to avoid catching or passing on an STD. Maybe, just maybe, you'll hear a bit about relationships and the emotions that often accompany sex. Lately, they probably teach you something about consent, too.

But sometimes schools don't even do this, and the sex education you get (if you get any) is a frantic list of don'ts and prohibitions based on *fears* around sex:

* Fear of young adults being sexual beings who might have sex outside of marriage.

* Fear of those who might identify outside the very limited spectrum of heterosexuality.

* Fear of those who, because of all the aforementioned possibilities, might get pregnant or worse still, might actually discover that sex is fun and pleasurable even when it occurs outside of marriage.

Our culture's conversation about consent also tends to be how-to oriented, and extremely basic. Maybe you've even seen the viral video "Tea Consent," which is basically a consent-for-dummies instructional video, where the narrator explains consent as offering one's partner tea and the partner either saying "yes, thank you", or saying they don't want the tea. The video advises that if a person says no to tea, the other shouldn't then pour the tea over their heads or force them to drink. Aka the basics of consent learned! Voilà!

Well, yeah. Sure. *Duh.*

The problem with this approach is that it literally dumbs down consent to technicalities, those "yeses" or "nos" people give (or don't give) in relation to it. And while *technically*, sure, those "yeses" and "nos" are important, to sum up consent like this grossly oversimplifies it. You don't get the kind of consent education that *you*—and everyone you know—needs.

Consent is about so much more than saying *yes* or *no*. It's about wants and desires and sexual fulfillment and intimacy and experimentation. It's about getting to give and experience the special kind of respect and care between you and your partner that sexual intimacy affords. Consent is about honesty—you being true to yourself and to your partner, and both being willing to share that truth with each other in some of the most vulnerable and wonderful circumstances available to us.

We do the same thing with sex: we tend to teach the technicalities of it rather than the meaning of it; we avoid pondering the nuances of sexuality, what makes a good relationship, what sex has to do with our humanity and the humanity of others. We teach the possible negative consequences while failing to mention the many, fabulous *positive* consequences like connection and pleasure and love and having an amazing time with our partners.

Within both sex and consent education, we usually avoid the very same Big Questions of Sex and Consent that this book is about. And while it's really important that you learn the technicalities and how-tos of sex and consent (how the body works, how you have sex, technically, how you prevent pregnancy and STIs, as well as the relationship between consent and the words *yes* and *no*), that is *not* why we're here.

We're here to let our imaginations run wild.

We're here to really and truly think through what it might mean to become a sexually liberated person who seeks out

sex-positive experiences and consensual, fulfilling relationships. We're here to take a leap of faith that maybe this lovely-
sounding utopia that I describe isn't as far off as it seems, and
might even be a little bit closer to reality if we all commit to
struggling through (and then struggling through some more)
the questions that frame the chapters that follow this one.

Who This Book Is For: EVERYBODY!!! (Yes, You! And You and You and *You!*)

I do *not* believe in a one-size-fits-all approach to sex and sexuality.

As in, everyone is supposed to do X. Or all people should feel
Y. Or the only good sex occurs in marriage. Or the right way to
do it is *that* way. Or, to be normal about sex is to be like *this*.
These kinds of sweeping pronouncements about how sex should
be or is supposed to be, those claims that this is how you are
supposed to feel about sex or when you have sex if you don't
react a certain way then something is wrong with you?

Get those shoulds and supposed-tos out of your head right
now.

It's not that you *shouldn't* listen to other people's opinions
about sex and consent, or that all opinions from others are
invalid. Obviously, you know I think it's important for you to
talk to other people about sex and get their opinions, to hear
what they have to say, since one of the first things I did in this
book is ask you to identify some conversation partners.

What worries me is when the shoulds and supposed-tos that

we get from culture, religion, and often very-well-meaning people end up repressing or taking away our impulse to figure out who we are as sexual beings. Those shoulds and supposed-tos can work together to turn sex and consent into a list of rights and wrongs that come from outside of specific people (like you) and particular relationships, as though there are universal laws about how to be sexual and gendered. These universalized "laws" and lists take *away* the responsibility for our own sex lives and sexualities from us—disempowering us in the process.

As I will continue to emphasize, being and becoming a sexual being is a big responsibility. As with any responsibility, we each need to shoulder that responsibility for ourselves and on behalf of our relationships. You, the reader, are coming to this book with ideas about sex and a long list of dos and don'ts that you've already acquired—even if you don't realize this yet. It's not as though I want you to completely forget those things—in fact, I want you to think long and hard about that list you've got (even if you can't quite pinpoint where you got it or how you got it). Part of this work involves analyzing that list and deciding where you are in relation to all those dos and don'ts that society, culture, religion, and adult people in our lives pass on to us.

The point of this book is to help you to figure out yourself—not to make you just fall in lockstep with how society tells you to be.

Whether the *you* that is reading this right now identifies as lesbian, gay, hetero, queer, asexual, trans, cis, nonbinary, Black, white, brown, olive, or something else, or some of the above, or none of the above, this book is inclusive of the *you* that you are and it's especially *for* the you that you are. This book is for people of some faith, a little faith, no faith, devout faith—and for Jews, Muslims, Hindus, Catholics, Christians, and all religions, too. This book isn't about *having* sex and *consenting* to sex now, this minute, and it isn't about denying that religious teachings around sex can offer guidance and value. It *is* about considering these hugely important subjects and asking serious questions about them. There is no timeline prescribed here for the *having sex* part, because that part can be as soon as tomorrow or a very long way off or never at all, depending on how *you*, the reader, puzzles through your own answers.

Atheists and agnostics, welcome! Democrats and Republicans and Independents, welcome! Come one, come all, because here within these pages, everyone is invited to enter.

YOU, most of all, are invited.

My intention is to help you build a framework and to acquire a set of tools that will help you forge your own path on these issues. I want you to have the critical thinking skills and the confidence to take the dos and don'ts that will come your way (and keep on coming for the rest of your life), and *evaluate them* according to your own set of beliefs, ethics, and feelings. My deepest wish is to help you discover an attitude toward sex, sexuality, and consent that fits *you* and respects those you care for.

This is a long process, something that takes time, work, and attention—not something that can happen overnight. Really, it's a process that should take a lifetime, because we are always in process, always becoming, always changing.

And the best time to start is now.

A Bit About Me Before We Move On
(Why Am I Writing This Book, Anyway?)

A few things you should know about me.

I'm a cisgender woman (more on that later), white, politically liberal, a progressive Catholic.

I'll clarify a bit on the Catholic front, since religious affiliation is a pretty universal flashpoint for all the issues in this book.

I'm Catholic, yes, *and* I'm pro-choice, *and* I'm pro-LGBTQ sex, relationships, and marriage in every way, shape, or form these might occur. I believe that sex outside the confines of marriage is often good, life-giving, affirming, and ethical. I am a social justice–oriented Catholic, and one who has a deep and abiding respect for its spiritual traditions. I also believe that the social justice and spiritual traditions of the world's religions (in general) have a tremendous amount to offer all of us in terms of determining why sex and consent are meaningful aspects of our humanity. There is a lot of good there. It's just that, unfortunately, most of what the world's religions— Catholicism and Christianity especially—have chosen to hammer at us are the negative, prohibitive aspects about sex that reside within their traditions. But there are many, many doorways into being a person of faith, and not all of them go through an obsession with the pelvis and the many ways that sex is sinful. Huzzah!

I've been talking about sex and consent and all that goes with these things for many years now to college students. I've done national studies and I give talks and do workshops on college campuses of all types across the United States. I've written books on all of the above. I'm a longtime advocate and activist on LGBTQ issues and sexual violence prevention.

Because of this advocacy and research and the thousands upon thousands of conversations, and after listening to college students reflect on these subjects from every angle imaginable, I've given a lot of thought to how best to approach the tasks of sex and consent education. About how we might try to do *this* instead of *that*, about what works toward the end of education and empowerment, and what really does not work, and winds up repressing a person, causing them shame, or even does the opposite of educate.

I've given a lot of thought to that sexually liberated utopia!

What's more, I've heard so many college students talk about *what they wish they had known* five or ten years ago about sex and consent. What they wish someone had told them about love, about relationships, about gender and sexuality. What they wish they could go back and tell their younger selves—if only they had the chance.

In my dreamiest of dreams, I want this book to fulfill those wishes.

I want you to have the benefit of all that wishing.

And I've spent well over a decade doing some wishing in my own right—wishing that kids might be offered a new approach to sex and consent education, one that takes a completely different tack toward this super important task.

So this book is *my* wish for you, too.

Journal, Journal, Journaling Is AWESOME!

One last thing I'll say in this introduction: As you work through the questions that follow, I'd like you to have a place where you can write down reflections, ideas, make lists, ponder your own thoughts and feelings, and revise those thoughts and feelings into something new after some more reflection. We are going to be framing each chapter with Big Questions, so it makes sense that you will want a space to put your answers—whether big, small, or somewhere in between—a place where you can mull over your uncertainties and wonderings.

I'd like you to keep a journal alongside your reading.

Think of it as a travel diary, but the travel involves the kind that you do in your heart and your mind, and through the conversations you have with people about the topics in this book—a record of this particular search for answers and understanding. A place to write down that list of names that I asked you to brainstorm for yourself, so that you'll always be able to remind yourself that, really, you are not alone in this.

You *could* use your phone or a tablet—you *could*. But I strongly suggest that you find a physical notebook, an object you can hold in your hands and open across your lap or your desk. The topics we are discussing require some unplugging to really get to the heart of how you feel about them—some uninterrupted focus and contemplation. A physical book is best for this I think, since it will free you from interruptions and distractions— because exploring Big Questions requires some devotion on your part.

Time to Get Crafty:

If you do decide to start a journal, find one that you like, that feels yours, that either you love at first sight or that you turn into something you love by making it your own. Decorate it, put stickers on it, write yourself an encouraging note on the very first page, put some drawings in the white space. Turn it into a fun and lovely art project!

Welcome, My Fellow Philosophers and Ethicists! Our Big Questioning Starts NOW!

Who Are YOU Anyway? Becoming a Critical Thinker ABOUT YOURSELF

The Big Questions and Why They Matter (To Sex! And Consent!)

Do you know who you are?

I don't just mean things like your name, address, age, racial identity, or even your gender (we'll come back to that one later). I am talking about who you are in the big picture. I'm talking about the Big Questions that give this book its name. Believe it or not, that's where this journey to figure out sex and consent begins.

Let me back up.

When I was in college, I majored in philosophy. I was on a search for "self." I gobbled up any and all theory and reading that might help me better figure out who I was and what it meant to live a meaningful life, a good life, a *human* life. I wanted to understand what was required of me to be a good (i.e., ethical) person. I wanted to understand myself (in general) and myself in relation to others (especially).

And I fell in love—deeply in love—with Big Questions.

Here are a few of those questions:

* Who am I and why am I here?

* What does it mean to be in the world?

* What do I believe and why?

* How do I find happiness and why do certain things make me happy or unhappy?

* What kind of a person do I hope to be in relation to others?

* What are my ethics and what do they require of me?

* What are my priorities?

* What factors make up my identity? (Race? Gender? Religion?)

* What gives life pleasure and why?

* Is there a God?

* Why are we here? Why am *I* here?

* What am I doing and why am I doing it?

I could keep going but I'll stop there.

I bet you have already asked yourself some of these questions, maybe even all of them. These are the kind of fundamental questions that we ask while we grow up, the Who and How and Why questions that drive our parents crazy because they don't have easy answers. These are questions that move writers to write, philosophers to philosophize, scientists to wonder and experiment. Questions that have given psychologists and therapists the stuff that keeps their offices full and their research going. They spark our minds and help us figure out what we want to do in our futures, what and who we love and don't, what paths we want to pursue and others we want to avoid.

Maybe you are already as deeply in love with Big Questions as I was back when I was just a little older than you are now.

But if you *haven't* asked these questions before, do not worry. This is the time to begin. The Big Questions that frame this book will help you on your own search for self, your search for what it means to be human, your search for relationships: good, fulfilling, and mutually respectful ones. Be they friendly or romantic or both.

It's time to add four more Big Questions to our list:

* What does it mean to be a sexual being?

* What is the meaning and purpose of sex?

* What is love?

* What is consent?

Trying to answer these questions is *not* going to be neat and tidy and easy. Life is just not that way, and neither are sex and consent. These are questions you will ask and return to for the rest of your lives. Each time you do, you may see them a little bit differently, or even have a different answer.

But be not afraid!

Once you open yourself to big, open-ended topics and questions—and to the wonder and contemplation and conversation they require—you also start getting comfortable with questions that don't have obvious responses. These questions stop being so daunting.

Big Questions point us toward what is most important and meaningful to us. They help us discover what it is to live a good and happy life, which also involves a life where we respect the good and worth of others. They are the very questions that turn us into critical thinkers—about ourselves.

Critical Thinking Is Not Just for School—Know Thyself, People!

If you haven't yet heard your teachers talk about critical thinking skills, get ready. During high school and college, the phrase "critical thinking" and the goal of developing "critical thinking skills" will be zinging all over the place, like some annoying, persistent fly that is really interested in your lunch.

Critical thinking is at the heart of Big Questioning.

It involves the ability to process and formulate ideas about a book or novel or essay that go beyond the mere summary of it, ideas that are informed by *other* knowledge you possess from *other* texts you've read, and *other* things you've experienced. Critical thinking is about putting together ideas and knowledge you've gotten from multiple places. It's about forming opinions because you've become a thinker about the many things you've read and lived through.

We often tell kids and young adults they need to become critical thinkers about what they read in school and learn in the news, but we don't often tell them they need to become critical thinkers *about themselves.*

More than anything, I want you to become a critical thinker about *yourself.*

Socrates, Plato's famous teacher-philosopher, passed along to Western history the notion that "the unexamined life is not worth living." This adage is practically a cliché by now (you can even find it printed on T-shirts at places like Urban Outfitters!). But cliché or no, I think these words are true. If you take the time to examine your life, if you *learn the skills* you need to be an examiner of yourself (a self-critic), your life will become more meaningful. I also believe that this examination of self—this critical thinking turned toward *you*—will not only help you, but its benefits will spill over into your relationships, too. True empowerment and respect for yourself involves working through your beliefs, your commitments, and your sense of ethics. It involves an *examination* of life, of self, of relationships and your role within them.

When you're a kid, you hear all the time that knowledge is power.

The thing is, knowledge really is power!

And critical thinking is one of the best paths toward knowledge.

So logically it follows: Critical thinking about *yourself* would also be a great path toward self-knowledge.

The more you ask Big Questions about aspects of life that don't have easy answers, the more you open up to critical thinking about yourself, your decisions, and your relationships, then the better equipped you'll be when you are facing this complicated, confusing, yet also beautiful and wonderful aspect of humanity that is your sexuality. And the closer you are to becoming an empowered, liberated person about sex and consent, the closer we all get to that sexually liberated utopia I was talking about earlier. And all the people we have relationships with will benefit from our honest and thoughtful approach to sex that goes way beyond just technicalities.

Figuring out sex and consent is really a conversation about who you are as a person and who you are as a person in relation to others. A *thinking* and *feeling* person. Someone whose heart and brain and body and soul are working in concert. (Just like Mozart.)

We Are Not Brains in a Vat! Reconnecting Our Hearts, Souls, and Bodies to Our Minds

(Get ready: here comes more philosophy.)

A philosopher of the Enlightenment, René Descartes, did a

lot of wondering and Big Questioning of the relationship between our brains and our bodies. To do this, Descartes wondered: What if I am just a brain in a vat? What if the rest of me isn't really here?

I'm a big fan of Descartes, but unfortunately, this kind of thinking—separating our brains and our thinking from the rest of our bodies—is problematic. It's *hierarchical* thinking. It values the mind *over* the body, the rational *over* the emotional, the individual *over* the relational. We grow up learning that the things worth thinking critically about are things like history, literature, sociology, politics, science. Our educations favor things we can *measure*, things we can know *unequivocally*, things we can know with *certainty*—things that *aren't* messy.

The stuff of our bodies, sex, relationships?

They can get pretty messy. Sometimes *really* messy.

So? We don't study these in the classroom much. Not in the same way that we study math and history and literature.

Therefore:

We aren't in the *habit* of critical thinking about this stuff.

We don't learn to use our wonderful brain skills to understand our matters of the heart, the desires, the body, the soul, and all that not-so-easily measurable stuff. It's a *bias* that infects our lives and our educations—and our understanding of sex and consent suffers as a result.

We need to *fix* this, people!

Fear not. I have good news.

We are going to reconnect our brains to our bodies and hearts and souls (we can do it!). All it takes is practice.

Thinking practice!!!!! (Yahoo!!!!)

Thinking practice is work, but I promise that this work is worth doing, and the Big Questions are here to help you *practice* this critical thinking about the complicated, messy, not-so-easily-measured stuff of life. I want you to practice being okay with the uncertainties that come with sex and desire and the tension these things bring to our lives (both positive and difficult).

Aristotle (yes, *another* philosopher) taught that when we *practice* certain activities they become *habits*. For him, habits and ethical behavior are connected. When we *practice* good things, we are building some serious (ethics) muscles.

Once *you* learn to flex your critical thinking muscle, you'll make it stronger.

And I want you to be super strong!

Becoming strong (and practiced!) in this way is one of the most important things you can ever do for yourself—and for every relationship in your life.

This means I am going to remind you, again and again, about critical thinking and how to do it, along with the kinds of practices and ideas and questions and connections that I eventually hope will become automatic to you. I want to *teach* you to become a critical thinker about the things your education might have left out so far—and may never teach you otherwise.

To learn to do this, involves realizing that your body, heart, and soul, and the particularities that make up you—like gender, sexual identity, and race—are not only *worth* thinking about but absolutely *necessary* to think about. It will change your life. I believe that with all my heart and soul and brain together. Learning this skill will prepare you in relation to sex and consent in ways that no amount of disembodied thinking and rote memorization and quantifiable, technical answers can do.

Because none of us are brains in a vat.

We're Gonna Party All Night (with Human Dignity)! Bringing Your BEST SELF out with You on the Weekend

I'll give you an example of what I want you to learn to do.

A lot of the talks about my research that I give at colleges are filled with students who care deeply about social justice—students concerned with human rights, with fostering a world that respects the dignity of all persons, and with confronting the conditions in which human rights and human dignity are unable to flourish. Many of these students are social justice *majors* and volunteer at homeless shelters and domestic violence shelters. They devote their spring breaks to building houses for those in need or working toward the goal of fostering human rights in another country.

Now.

If I ask an audience filled with college students if they care about social justice—every hand in the room will fly up. (Of course we care about social justice, Dr. Freitas!!!!!!!) If I ask that same audience how many of them care about human dignity—once again, every hand in the room will be in the air. (Yeah, *duh*, Dr. Freitas!!!!!)

However.

If I ask those students another question—one with a bit of a twist—suddenly those students in the room are stumped. "So," I'll say. "Where is the human dignity at the parties you go to on Friday night?"

I know. I *know*. It's just a slight shift, right?

Kind of like a simple math equation:

Human Dignity + Friday Night College Party = . . .

You'd think the answer might be super easy. Especially since most college students are very experienced and knowledgeable in partying hard on Friday nights (and on Thursdays and Saturdays, too).

But it rarely occurs to anyone to wonder why—if they are working hard to foster human dignity where they volunteer across the street from campus—it might also be important to practice those values with one another at the parties they attend right there at home.

With that one little question, suddenly everyone is able to see the *disconnect* between what they practice and value during the day in their studies and activities, and how they act toward each other at night when they are going out and being social. They realize what a *problem* it is when all this stuff is disconnected— how badly we may treat one another and treat our own bodies, how dangerous and problematic our behavior might become when we check our values and commitments at the door of the frat house.

To translate my question to college students another way:

Why aren't you bringing your VERY BEST SELVES to the party?

Why are you becoming SOMEONE ELSE when you go out at night?

I want to be clear: I am not blaming these students for this separation between their daily, classroom-sitting, thinking, volunteering, caring bodies and brains and their nighttime drinking, partying, sex-having, and hooking-up bodies and selves.

So where does the disconnect come from?

Well, it's kind of a failure in our educations. No one has explicitly *invited* those students to wonder about human dignity in relation to their partying, drinking, having-sex lives before. No one has told them how important it is to bring their best, critically thinking, human-dignity-caring selves out with them on Fridays and Saturdays.

So throughout this book, I am planning on sending you some super-explicit invitations. (Super-sexy, right?) I want this weird math that involves you putting skills and values and beliefs together with your social and relational practices and identities, math that turns you into a critical thinker about yourself, to become *automatic*. Natural. As easy and obvious as $2 + 2 = 4$.

Let's Take the Big Questions Outside!

1. Pick one of the Big Questions from pages 28–29.
Now take a walk somewhere you like, or a run, or a wander
(make sure to leave your smartphone at home). Devote your walk
to pondering your Big Question (we can all be like Socrates!). When
you come home, spend some time journaling about the thoughts
that went through your brain as you walked or jogged or wandered
(or kicked around the soccer ball or shot baskets, etc.).

2. Add new questions of your own to the list of Big Questions.
There are so many! Don't be afraid to think Big with the Questions
you have about life.

What Is My Relational Ethic?
Understanding Friendship

The Best and Worst of Friends: Three Lists

Ask yourself this:

What does it mean to be a good friend?

I am certain that this question automatically sparks answers to pop up in your brain. You *know*, instinctively, what good friendship is. You *know* because you've been a good friend yourself and you've had good friends in your life. And I am guessing, *hoping*, that you have good friends in your life right now, this minute.

And yeah, yeah, I *know*. You might be wondering:

Why am I asking about friendship in a book about sex and consent?

While you may not yet be sexually active, I am *certain* you have vast amounts of experience with friendship (both positive and negative). Your experience and the knowledge that comes with it is going to become essential, crucial, *foundational* to the thinking we're going to do about sex and consent that comes later. It's going to become the scaffolding for your *relational ethic*.

In order to examine this important question—What does it mean to be a good friend?—I want you to make three lists to help you think critically about friendship, when friendship is good, and when it is not so good and why.

LIST #1

Make a list of good friend qualities and actions. What examples can you think of in your own life where you've acted as a good friend?

Is good friendship about going to sit with that lonely person in the cafeteria, or about someone offering a bit of company when you are all alone at school? Is it about inviting someone to your house because you like them and want to spend more time with them? Is a good friend someone who makes you laugh? Someone who will keep a secret when you tell them one?

Think about the times that someone else has been a good friend to you. What did they do that signaled they were a good friend? Is it the smile on their face when they first see you arrive at school? Are they a person who not only sits next to you in class but also invites you to their house to hang out or even to sleep over now and then?

* What *actions* describe what good friends do?

* What *feelings* do good friends produce in you?

* What *feelings* does being a good friend to others produce in you?

LIST #2

Make a list of expectations for good friendship. I want you to think about the kinds of things you *expect* of your friends and what they *expect* of you.

For example, on my own list are qualities such as:

* A friend is a person who *listens*.

* A friend is someone who *makes me laugh*.

* A friend is someone who *spends time* with me—and who *makes time* for me.

* A friend is someone who *respects me* and my feelings.

* A friend is someone who *reminds me* that the world is a good place to be.

*An important note as you do this:

Sometimes we are taught that having expectations of other people is not a good idea, because people can disappoint you. Or we are taught that when other people have expectations of us, this is annoying because it places a burden on us, or it constricts our freedom. Or maybe we've been told that if we need things from others, this makes us *weak* or *clingy* or *dependent* instead of *independent*. Maybe you've been taught that admitting you need things from others is a negative.

If writing down expectations makes you feel uncomfortable or concerned that expectations of others make you weak or clingy or annoying, I want you to:

* *notice* these feelings—acknowledge that they are there.

* *sit with* these feelings—just let yourself have them.

Okay.

Now I want you to give yourself *permission* to be honest about the things you want from others, the ways you wish other people, your friends, would act and do and feel for you, even if you do your best to keep these things secret most of the time—maybe even from yourself. It's okay and necessary for good relationships to involve wanting and needing things from others. Try to let go of the voices in your head that tell you it's *not* okay or it means something is *wrong* with you. Learning to get comfortable with our expectations of others, and theirs of us, is an important part of understanding friendship and relationships in general.

LIST #3

Make a list of things that define a bad friend. I bet there are moments in your own life when you've been a not-so-good friend to someone and, likewise, there are people from school or your neighborhood who haven't been very nice to you. I bet answers and examples are already popping up in your head. You know what being treated poorly feels like deep in your gut—and you remember when and how you've done it to others deep in that gut, too.

Right?

Maybe you turned your back on someone who was trying to talk to you in the hallway at school. Maybe someone you thought was a friend saw you alone in the cafeteria and kept on walking as though you didn't exist. Maybe someone had a birthday party, invited people over to their house, or planned an outing and intentionally didn't invite you.

* What *actions* describe what bad friends do?

* What *feelings* do bad friends produce in you?

* What *feelings* does acting like a bad friend produce in you?

Here come some even more complicated questions:

* How do you know the difference between good and bad friendship—what signs can you think of?

* Does the term "bad friendship" even make any sense to you? Can you call someone who acts that way a friend at all?

* How can you be *sure* if someone is a good friend or not—is that even possible?

The answers to these questions might not be so obvious. You might realize in your ponderings that sometimes a friend (and yourself *as* a friend) can be good, and sometimes can be bad, too. That friendship is complicated and that friends can do wonderful things in our life, and sometimes they can disappoint us, too.

If you feel uncertain, if you're not sure how to feel about someone or even how to feel about yourself in relation to friendship, just like I asked you above—I want you to sit with those feelings. Simply let yourself *be* with this uncertainty. These questions are not easy to answer and that is totally okay.

Figuring Out Your Relational Ethic

Right in the lists you've created is the foundation for your very own relational ethic. The cornerstone!

These lists articulate *your* basic sense of right and wrong in relation to others: What *you* believe you should do, how you should act, how you should treat people and make them feel, and in turn, how they should do all of the above with you.

You've been developing this set of beliefs about relationships, a sense of right and wrong, this list of dos and don'ts since you were small—even if you didn't realize it. You have *already been practicing* relational ethics *your entire life!* You hold strong beliefs about how relationships should and shouldn't go, even if there is still uncertainty floating around in there. Many these beliefs come from what our families, teachers, faith traditions, coaches, and mentors teach us, and what the books we read teach us. But these beliefs also come from what our own experience teaches us—the ups and downs of life and being in relationships with others.

Today, you wrote them down so you can consider them on the page.

You made what *you* believe about friendship *explicit.*

You *articulated* this out loud. (Go you!)

Keep these lists with you, hold yourself to them, commit yourself to them. Your relational ethic is one of the best resources you have to teach and remind yourself of who and how you want to be in the world. We are going to be examining how these beliefs have been informed by the people in your life and the experiences you've had with others, and where you disagree with what you've been taught. We'll also be identifying some of the things that might be missing or that shouldn't be there in the first place. As you move through life, your list of beliefs about relationship ethics will expand and grow, get crossed out and revised, just as your experience of others and the world expands and grows and changes, too.

Getting COMFORTABLE with Ethics

One last thing. I want to talk to you about this word *ethics.*

I'm sure it's a word you know. Maybe you've heard it in school or at home with your parents or within your religious tradition if you have one. Maybe you are a budding philosopher and you've already spent a good deal of your young life reading Aristotle and Kant and Martha Nussbaum and their ideas about ethics before you go to sleep at night. (Or instead of going to sleep at night!)

Or maybe you've never before had a conversation about ethics, at least not one where the word *ethics* is used so explicitly. In my opinion, we don't talk about ethics enough. Sometimes we seem to be *allergic* to the idea of ethics, especially relational and sexual ethics (more on this again in the chapter on sexual ethics). And yet, we need to understand ethics when it comes to sex and consent. Both sex and consent depend on a combination of our personal relational ethic and also society's relational ethic (and all the other relational ethics that our culture and religions pass on and impose on us).

If we are to become people empowered and respectful around sex and consent, then developing our relational ethic is essential.

Without a sense of our own ethical attitude toward others (beginning with those close to us, like our friends, our parents, our family), sex and consent will continue to be these things that don't have much meaning or pleasure in our lives, that we don't have much control over. Not knowing what we believe and feel about sex and consent can disempower and even hurt or endanger us, or put us in situations where we can hurt and disempower and endanger others. Without a relational ethic, sex can become this thing that other people tell us to do or not do, or tell us is meaningless (even if we don't believe that). Without self-knowledge, we can feel powerless about sex, and consent can get reduced to two measly words—*yes* and *no*—if it gets considered at all.

I don't want this for you or for anyone.

I want you to *care deeply* about sex and consent, about all the good, the energy, connection, and pleasure a person can have around these issues. For that, you need to engage in the work that is relational ethics—work that will naturally lead you to sexual ethics and *also* to consent. Because you've already done the friendship lists described here, you are off to a good start. (Hooray for you!)

Make Time for Ethical Talk:

Sit down with one of your parents, your guardian, or an older sibling, and ask them to make those three lists that you just made. Walk them through making these lists, just like I walked you through it. Then, discuss your lists and their lists—what are the differences between them? Is there something on this other person's list that you'd like to add to yours? Or that you think maybe you should cross off yours? How are they different? Similar? Why do you think that is?

Now do the same thing with a friend your age, or even a couple of friends. Repeat as many times as you like, with as many people you feel comfortable talking to about this!

ADVICE TO OUR YOUNGER SELVES PART I

In honor of all the many students I've spoken to over the years who have talked of what they wished they could go back and tell their younger selves about sex, consent, and all its related topics, I asked some wonderful writers (some of whom you may already know! And some of whom I am happy to introduce you to if you don't!) what they would go back and tell their younger selves about the topics in this book. Starting here and in special sections you'll encounter through-out, this is what they told me—and they told me on behalf of *you*.

"Eliot, right now you probably feel a little small and soft and sexless, especially compared to some of the other kids in your grade. And that's fine! Truth is, there are a lot of different ways to be gay. Porn will give you the impression of 'this is how people are supposed to do it,' and being maybe a little too type-A, you'll fight hard to fulfill expectations. Don't fight so hard, except for the fight to be yourself. Real sexual intimacy with another guy will bloom when you com-municate well with yourself—and him—about what you want. And it doesn't have to be what it seems like the rest of the gay world is doing."

—ELIOT SCHREFER, author of the Ape Quartet and Lost Rainforest series

"Hey Javi, listen, I'm not going to tell you that this thing you are feeling, this explosive force of wanting is not the real thing. It's love all right. Just because you're twelve doesn't mean you can't experience true love. In many ways, what you are feeling now is truer than lots of stuff I felt when I was thirty-five. I want you to take a few moments to experience what is true and genuine about what you are feeling. Inside this energy, can you detect the *giving* that is in it, the desiring to make another person happy? Can you feel the respect for who she truly is in what you are feeling? You want her to love you back so badly, but you realize that her love must be given freely. Her loving you is up to her. I know you are afraid that she will find you unworthy and if she does, you will hurt, there's no denying that. But this I can tell you from my old-age: if your love is a giving and not a taking, you will be loved, truly and freely loved."

-FRANCISCO X. STORK, author of *Disappeared* and *Marcelo in the Real World*

"Dear 12-year-old self: I know you desperately want to be seen and to talk to someone, anyone, about all the feelings you're having lately. I wish you didn't have to push them all down deep inside you because you've been told you're not supposed to have these kinds of feelings. But it's perfectly okay to have them and there's nothing wrong with you. It's confusing when all you hear is that good girls don't think about sex, let alone talk about it. But then adult men look at you or touch you in a certain way and it makes you feel uncomfortable. And you're afraid to tell anyone because you know they won't believe you. But it's not your fault. You're not the sick one here. You'll find the strength and it's going to get better."

-SABINA KHAN, author of *Zara Hossain Is Here* and *The Love and Lies of Rukhsana Ali*

"You are alone with a girl you like and you are nervous (let's face it, scared) and even though you think looking and sounding like someone who hasn't done this before will make you look stupid, and that she'll make fun of you, and she'll tell everyone else, and then they'll make fun of you—pretending you know everything isn't going to help. Here's what pretending you know everything does: it makes it all about *you*, and if you are about to kiss a girl, or even later, if you are about to have sex with a girl, if you are making it all about you, you are ignoring the other person in the equation. How can you claim to care about a person if you are ignoring her? Even though it is scary, even though you are afraid you'll sound dumb, the smart thing, the right thing, the thing that will help you be a better kisser, a better sexual partner, a better person (than a faker who is pretending) is to talk first, and ask questions: can I kiss you? can I kiss you here? When you are alone with the girl you like, ignore all the things your friends have said, ignore all the things you've seen on TV, and just ask her. You don't have to pretend, she's probably nervous too, and that's okay! You can be nervous together! And what's best is that if you are both honest with each other, you'll probably become a little less nervous together."

–BRENDAN KIELY, author of *Tradition* and *The Last True Love Story*

"When I was 12 years old, I was still playing with dolls and Lego. And that's okay too. You may not be ready to think about sex and sexual relationships. File this information away in your mind for future reference, but don't feel you have to look or act a certain way because of a number (your age) or because that's what everyone else is doing. You'll know when you're ready. Enjoy the place where you are now and the people who are there with you."

–LYN MILLER-LACHMANN, coauthor of *Moonwalking* and
author of *Rogue*

"Dear Alex, I know you want to be wanted. I know you want to be held. I know you want to kiss a guy and feel his touch. You'll have all that one day. I know you feel you can't wait—and no matter what I say, you're going to do what you're going to do. And you'll do some things you'll later regret. There will be people who love you, until they don't. And people you love, until you don't. Your heart will be broken, and you'll pick up the pieces and put them back together. Things will seldom turn out like you dreamed. There will be times when you feel you can't go on. But you'll live and learn from your experiences, both good and bad. And despite your mistakes, you'll make it through. Just never give up. You'll have other dreams come true—better than you ever imagined. I promise."

—ALEX SANCHEZ, author of *You Brought Me the Ocean* and *Rainbow Boys*

"Hey Raf, You're going to learn that one of the worst things about sex and sexuality is that everyone makes it so hard to talk about. It's always either funny or embarrassing or taboo, and the end result is that you don't hear what you need to hear. There is so much stigma about sex. Especially in Texas. Especially in the 90s. Especially when you're 12. I want you to ignore that to the best of your ability. You dodged a bullet by being born into a liberal family but, kiddo, that's not enough. Sex is still weirdly intertwined with shame in your mind. But nothing you feel or want is weird, or gross, or awful, or perverted. It'll seem that way, and you'll find yourself moving from one shame spiral to the next, for a full 25 years. Once you finally realize masturbation is normal, you'll worry about being gay. Once you get over the gay thing, you'll worry about wanting to have sex before love. Then the next thing, and the next, until you're approaching forty. Why waste that much time worrying about sex? Why let people you never met and certainly never cared about dictate the terms of your sexuality to you? Just be you, Raf. Cheers, Approaching Forty Raf."

—RAFI MITTLEFEHLDT, author of *What Makes Us* and *It Looks Like This*

PART ONE

Let's Talk About Sex, Baby!

(Let's Talk About YOU and ME!)

What Is SEXUAL IDENTITY?

The Heterosexism Problem and the Idea of the Closet

Imagine a world where, as we grow up, our parents, the people around us who raise and teach us, help us learn to wonder who we might turn out to love as we get older.

Will we be attracted to girls?

Will we be attracted to boys?

Both? Neither?

Will we be attracted to all genders? To everybody imaginable, regardless of how they identify?

You might already be living in a home or a community where people are asking these kinds of questions. If you are, that's wonderful.

I'd love to see that kind of world everywhere. For everybody!

But for now, many of us grow up under very particular

assumptions about our sexuality: that we are *heterosexual*. To be more specific, that your *sexual identity* (which is determined by who we are romantically attracted to) is heterosexual.

This means that if you identify as a boy, then you will be attracted to girls, and if you identify as a girl, you will be attracted to boys. We live in a "heterosexist" culture and society, which means that pretty much all children and all people are *assumed* to be heterosexual—until and unless you identify otherwise and decide to tell this to the world.

This is where we get the idea of the "closet" and the phrase you likely already know: "coming out" or "coming out of the closet."

Most people assume that everyone is heterosexual—because heterosexuality is still our society's *default* sexual identity. And most people also assume that *not* being heterosexual is something to hide. That if a person knows they are not heterosexual, then they will and should feel ashamed, embarrassed, even horrified.

Hence the closet—a place where you can keep your identity hidden, in the dark, behind a closed door.

It's not that all closets are bad, or that shutting yourself away (cloistering yourself) for privacy's sake or to think on something is a problem. Privacy, wanting to be alone with something for a bit, keeping something to yourself, is totally okay. Privacy is a good and important thing and you have the right to it. But there is a difference between choosing to be alone to think and to ponder—to cloister yourself, which I am a fan of—and believing it necessary to *hide* in a closet because society teaches you to be ashamed of who you are.

How I would love to abolish *this* closet! How I would love to abolish the *need* for the closet, so people could stay and feel safe!* And all the hiding, shame, and difficulty we place on anyone who doesn't follow this societal "norm" of heterosexuality!

The only thing your sexual identity has to do with is who and whether you feel inclined to love, who you feel attraction for, who you get crushes on, and who you kind of maybe *like-like*. Those feelings are completely and totally positive and wonderful. Those feelings are feelings we should celebrate. Those feelings are some of the ones that make life good and happy and meaningful. The more of those feelings, the merrier! It doesn't matter if you are heterosexual, gay, lesbian, bisexual, asexual, or otherwise. You love who you love who you love however you love, and this love is good and something to be proud of—and not at all something to hide.

---

* I also want to be clear: if you are in the closet right now, and if you are not ready (not even *nearly* ready) to come out, there is *nothing wrong* with this. There is nothing wrong with *you*. Something is wrong with *society*. People stay in the closet for very good reasons: for safety because they fear a community's, parents', friends' reaction to their sexual identity or because they do not yet have the necessary support network for coming out. It's absolutely okay to stay safe until you feel supported and ready—I want your safety above all else.

Why Is Sexual Identity and Being Heterosexual Such a Big Deal?

You might be wondering why we live in such a heterosexist world.

Why do people *assume* everyone is heterosexual?

Why is it such a big deal to *not* identify as heterosexual? So big that there are rehab-like "conversion therapy" facilities in some states that attempt to turn LGBTQ people heterosexual. (Because conversion therapy is so harmful and abusive, it is illegal for minors in eighteen states, including California, Oregon, and Washington, as well as all of New England, New York, and New Jersey. I'd like to see it illegal everywhere and for everyone, including adults.)

Why should anybody *ever* be ashamed of who they love?

Like, how in the world did we get here?

These are very good questions. The answers are complicated.

There are all sorts of reasons why our world is this way, most of which have to do with fear, and most of which are, ultimately, irrational. So many thinkers and philosophers (including Plato) imagine our sexuality on a continuum (which is like one big line) where there are many degrees of sexual identity. Identifying as *exclusively* and *extremely* heterosexual is pretty unusual (at the one end of this line), but our culture pushes all of us toward heterosexuality. So a majority of people grow up to express themselves as heterosexual, which in turn allows society and culture to affirm heterosexuality as the norm. (Statistics around how much of the population identifies as heterosexual vary greatly depending on a person's country. I wonder how these statistics will start to vary just we are beginning to live in a world where people are more open to LGBTQ people.)

Identifying as anything other than the norm is always tough.

Norms are tough in general and norms to do with sex and sexual identity are especially problematic. As I've said before, there is no one-size-fits-all approach to sex and sexuality.

But our culture and society and certainly our religious traditions tend to preach that there *is* such a thing as one-size-fits-all sexuality and to promote this one-size-fits-all approach as utterly essential. They teach that there is a "normal" way to have sex and be a sexual being and that there are "abnormal" or "wrong" ways to have sex and be a sexual being. Sometimes culture, society, and religions will try to convince *everyone* this is true as if the future of our world's existence depends on everyone and their mothers and fathers and grandkids and cousins believing this truth even if it destroys all of us to do so.

Unfortunately, there are still many people in our world who believe that to identify as LGBTQ is abnormal and even wrong. Because our world favors the norm that is heterosexuality, we still have prohibitions about being LGBTQ—again, hence the closet.

So, *why* is this norm based on people's fears and biases still around?

I hate to say this but:

One *big* reason is religion.

Societal and institutional systems often survive on maintaining certain norms and universal beliefs, and worry that they will die or break apart if those norms and beliefs are disrupted and start to change. Religions especially worry about continuity—perpetuating traditions and passing them on to the next generation—and heterosexuality is one of the norms religions *especially* worry about. Our culture, society, and religions have very particular ideas about what makes a "family" and what makes a "stable family"—one man, one woman, plus children. These institutions see sexual identities *other than* heterosexuality as problematic to this notion of family and threatening to their own survival.

Yeah. I know. Complicated. And this is just the beginning.

As a person of faith myself, I find it tragic that the world's religions are so anti-LGBTQ. Christianity, which is still the tradition of the majority of Americans, is particularly anti-LGBTQ (at least officially—there are always plenty of Christians who disagree with this in practice).

There *are* Christian denominations that have departed from this position (one prominent example is Unitarian Universalism). Within most Christian denominations and certain other religious traditions like many liberal Jewish communities, you can find factions tolerant of, embracing of, and pro-LGBTQ. The Methodist Church, for example, has been famously divided over admitting LGBTQ people and ministers, as has the Episcopal Church, which split in two because of divisions over related issues. And members of the Church of Jesus Christ of Latter-day Saints have wavered slightly of late on the subject of LGBTQ people after a slew of tragic suicides among LGBTQ-identifying young adult Mormons.

But, even though if you dig deeply enough you are likely to

find religious people—be they Christian, Catholic-Christian, Jewish, Muslim, Hindu, and so on—who are open and loving toward LGBTQ people, and who identify proudly as LGBTQ, the main reason our world is so difficult to live in if you are LGBTQ is because of religions. Anti-gay legislation in the US generally originates from within religious circles. Anti-gay movements and demonstrations and anti-LGBTQ lawsuits come from within religious quarters, too.

Your church or mosque or synagogue or religious community might be divided over this issue. Or it may have taken a clear stance one way or the other—to be open and tolerant, or to be closed and intolerant. I hope that your community, if you have one, is open.

I long for our world and its religions to open their hearts and minds. I want our world to be a loving place for anyone who loves and for however they choose to love. I want the world to celebrate loving of any and all types because *love* and *like* and *attraction* are good. Period. And if you have any faith at all, this is one of the things that I want you to have faith in.

Who Do You Love?

Do *you* know who you are attracted to yet?

Do you know what your sexual identity is yet?

It's totally okay if you don't. It's totally okay if you never settle on one thing or the other, too, and if your sexuality is in flux. Questioning one's sexuality, trying to figure out who you are attracted to, discovering that you feel attraction to this person but not that person, or these people but not those people, is an exciting, wonderful part of growing up, of being a young adult, of being a *human person*. It also can be totally confusing! And daunting! And make us really nervous! (Because what if the person we're attracted to doesn't like us back? Or (!!!)! What if they *do* like us back!!!! What then?! (OMG!!))

Who we are attracted to can change over time. You might fall in love with a girl today and girls for the next ten years, and then discover when you turn thirty or thirty-five or when you are fifty or even seventy that you are in love with a man and are attracted to men. Which is totally okay! All kinds of things change as we get older and sometimes one of those things is who we are attracted to and how and why. Attraction doesn't have to be fixed and it's all right if it isn't fixed for you.

What I wish *with all my heart* is that you are living in a home and a community and among friends who will celebrate you and your sexual identity, no matter what it turns out to be or how you might question it and how it might shift over time. Whether you are gay, lesbian, heterosexual, bisexual, asexual, or another identity, or you think of your sexual identity as fluid, ever-changing, and absolutely outside of all categories.

I'll repeat this here because I want this to sink in and sink in deeply:

There is no one-size-fits-all way to be a sexual person.

The only important thing is that you have the freedom and support to figure out who *you* are as a sexual person. That you have people around you who will affirm whatever you discover. That you know with all your heart that you are *not* alone in this.

If you are not living with people and in a place that will celebrate you no matter what, I want you to know this: You are still not alone. You have me, the writer of this book, for one. And there are many other people nearby and in this world who will be there to support and affirm you—even if you can't see them right now, this minute. I promise we exist. We are here, you will find us, and we are never that far away.

However they identify, every person who exists—if they hope to be empowered in their sexuality—*must give some thought* to who they are attracted to and why. Reflection, contemplation, and critical thinking about this question will only help us become more self-aware about who we are. Just because you identify as heterosexual does not mean you are exempt from this pondering.

I repeat: you are not exempt, you heterosexual people out there!

Of the college students I've met during my research, the most sexually self-aware and empowered and practiced critical thinkers are those who identify as LGBTQ. The world we live in has forced them to think about these issues precisely *because* they fall outside of heterosexist norms.

This also means that the *least* empowered and the *least* sexually self-aware people tend to be those who identify as heterosexual. Societal norms allow heterosexual people to get away with not thinking about their sexuality. While this might be convenient, it's definitely not a good thing. Most heterosexual people have a lot of catching up to do when it comes to understanding themselves as sexual beings. (So get going, then, if that describes you! Yes, *you*!)

Take Some Personal Time:

1. Spend some time journaling about your own sexual identity. Whether you are sure or not, it's okay if you don't know—and it's okay if you do, too!

2. Consider talking to someone you trust about your sexual identity. Regardless of whether you are sure of your identity or whether you are questioning, it's good to think about who you are attracted to and why and to talk about it with someone you trust. Just because you might not have a closet to worry about doesn't mean you don't have to think about your sexual identity.

What Is Gender and Gender Identity?

Biology versus Sex versus Masculinity versus Femininity versus Gender

If you follow the news, you've probably heard something about the gender identity debates that keep happening in our culture. These debates extend to all sorts of things, from who gets to use which public and school bathrooms, to whether or not transgender people are allowed to serve in the military, to more basic questions about whether or not gender is culturally constructed or tied to a person's biology or even divinely ordained. These debates tend to be rooted in the broader question of whether we are *born* as women and men (if being a woman or a man is "nature") or if *we become* women and men because of culture and how we are raised (if being a woman or a man is "nurture").

If you are a person who does not neatly fit and/or resists our culture's normative gender roles of masculine or feminine, man or woman, chances are you've tuned in to these gender debates as you've gotten older because they affect you directly. (And because maybe they make you really, really angry.)

First, let's go over the basics and terminology.

What Do *Male* and *Female* Refer To?

These terms refer to biological sex and the reproductive organs and genitalia you were assigned at birth. These have to do with the physical and genetic characteristics of your body. We are talking penises and vaginas here, people!

What About *Intersex?*

Some people are born with both male and female reproductive organs, or have bodies that don't neatly fit the biological definitions of *male* and *female* and the term for this is *intersex.*

What Do *Masculine* and *Feminine* Refer To?

These terms have to do with gender, and a person's gender identity, and the normative traits and behaviors we associate with masculinity and femininity.

What counts as masculine and feminine in Western culture has to do with the way we stereotype or normalize these concepts—they are culturally conditioned (that is, created by culture, not by biology or nature). Stereotypes about what is masculine might include playing sports like football, having big muscles and a deep voice, wearing pants, having short hair, liking the color blue. Likewise, stereotypes about what is feminine might mean wearing a dress and makeup, painting one's fingernails, having long hair, and liking the color pink. (Remember: These are all stereotypes!*)

What Is *Trans* or *Transgender*?

A transgender person is someone who does not identify in terms of the gender traits typically associated with the biological sex they were assigned at birth. For example, someone who is assigned male at birth, but who identifies as a girl in terms of gender traits (a *trans woman*), or someone who is assigned female at birth, but who identifies as a man in terms of gender traits (a *trans man*). Being trans doesn't make anyone less of a boy or a girl or a man or woman, if that is how they identify.

When a baby is born, they have no control over whether they are assigned as *male* or as *female*, but as they grow up, they may begin to identify differently. There are also trans people who don't identify as men or women but who feel like a little bit of both or neither or in between.

---

* If you happen to fit these stereotypes, that's okay! Stereotypes aren't bad, in and of themselves. The problem with stereotypes is that they can be limiting and confusing—especially if you don't fit them neatly.

What Is *Nonbinary*?

A nonbinary person is someone who doesn't identify as a boy or man or girl or woman, with either gender, any gender, or who might identify with all genders, or a combination of genders. Some nonbinary people will also identify as trans, and some nonbinary people will not. Nonbinary people may also identify as *genderqueer* or just *queer* or as *gender nonconforming*.

What Is *Cisgender*?

A cisgender person (which is how I identify) is a person whose gender identity is the same as the biological sex they were assigned at birth. For example, biologically I am female, and I also identify as a woman.

There are more terms than the ones I've listed here—and new terms for identity will likely continue to arise as our culture and individuals work to find the right terminology and labels for a diversity of identities. When in doubt, just ask someone which label they prefer. People appreciate it when you ask—and if you don't understand what the label signifies, ask them to tell you.

Beware the Gender Police!

Because of its culture and the influence of religions, the United States is pretty conservative when it comes to raising children. What I mean is that if you were assigned male at birth, you were likely raised in a way that favors masculine stereotypes (maybe your bedroom was blue and you played baseball and you were given trucks and cars and Legos as presents as a kid). Likewise, if you were born female, you were likely raised in a way that favors feminine stereotypes (maybe your bedroom was pink and purple, with ruffled bedspreads and curtains, and you were given dolls and tutus and princess dresses).

Or maybe you have parents who actively resisted cultural stereotypes about girls and boys and the colors of your bedroom were more neutral (maybe yellows and greens), and your parents tried to make sure people didn't "gender" you in terms of the presents they gave you (you were just as likely to get trucks and Legos as tutus and dolls). Perhaps your parents encouraged you to grow your hair long and wear dresses if you wanted to even though you are a boy.

The traits, qualities, and preferences that we associate with a person's sex assigned at birth are completely arbitrary! (They change depending on the times and trends.) For example, it used to be that all small children, even boys, wore white dresses (yes, dresses!). And did you know that until the mid-twentieth century the color pink used to be a boy color? Pink was associated with blood, and blood was associated with being a warrior, so wearing pink made you a tough-as-nails warrior guy. (I know, shocking!) Our association of pink with girls is a relatively new trend.

Because you probably go to school with other kids and because current trends in gender stereotypes are so strong in our culture, it's unlikely you've escaped being gendered by the majority of people in your life. Even if your parents tried to resist the Disney Princess obsession for you, you may have ended up wanting princess outfits and wands and fluffy pink everything anyway. The same goes for boys who love to wear their hair long and wear skirts and dresses when they are little, but with cultural pressure to conform to masculine stereotypes, are discouraged from continuing to do this as they got older.

What you need to know is that the prescription that boys can't wear dresses and skirts or paint their toenails or do ballet is literally just this—a cultural norm or trend, nothing more. There's no ultimate or natural law that prohibits boys from wearing a dress or painting their toenails with glitter! The same goes for girls who want to play with trucks or cut their hair close to their scalps or play football. Nature doesn't require girls to have long hair. It's only a cultural preference that teaches girls this!

Even so, depending on where you live, these preferences can be strictly enforced. While it might seem harmless on the surface (Who really cares if a boy wants to wear a pink tutu? Who really cares if a girl wants to ride a dirt bike instead of play with dolls? I mean, it's not like this is going to hurt anybody!), there are people in our world who care deeply about conforming to gender stereotypes. A lot of people are invested in you, the person reading this, looking and acting like the cultural stereotype of a boy or a girl.

Why? you are wondering. *Why* is this the way that it is?

Well. As with heterosexuality, the world's religions are (generally) very invested in there being only two genders, masculine and feminine, which correspond according to male and female biology. Many religious people believe that gender as it corresponds to biology is divinely ordained: as in, ordered and created by God. They believe that the perpetuation of life depends on this, and according to certain religions, so does a person's salvation and afterlife. They believe that to defy one's gender and to break out of these gender norms is to defy God, to live a life of sin, to turn one's back on future salvation, and is therefore prohibited.

I predict people strongly invested in cis men only using men's restrooms and cis women only using women's restrooms are likely also strongly religious and strongly anti-LGBTQ (even though lots of trans folk pass so completely that they would likely startle people if they *didn't* use the bathroom associated with their gender identity!). Some people police gender as though their lives and the entire world's salvation depend on this (and this is what they might even believe). Many religions even go so far as to regulate how women and men can and cannot dress and even when and where and with whom they are allowed to appear (or not appear) in public. Some traditions will tolerate a certain amount of gender-bending, and plenty of people within the world's religions may disagree with and even defy the gender norms of their tradition, just as they might defy heterosexist norms about sexual identity.

But sometimes the price of that defiance can be life-threatening.

I tell you this not to frighten you but because it is the truth. The stakes are sometimes that high for people who defy gender norms.

If you have parents who are not worried about you being LGBTQ and who are not convinced that masculine and feminine stereotypes are divinely ordained, then gender-bending and resisting these norms is probably totally fine in your house. Maybe you live in a house where if you were biologically assigned as a boy yet you feel like a girl and eventually you identify as a transgender girl/woman, your parents and siblings are good with that! My hope is that your family celebrates the person you are, whatever your gender identity turns out to be.

There are plenty of people in our world—maybe your own parents and maybe even you—who couldn't care less who uses which bathroom! Or who grows their hair long or plays which sport or likes which color! Hooray! I'd love us all to strive to make the world a place where it doesn't matter who uses which bathroom or which colors to paint our rooms or no one minds how we cut and style our hair. We have more important things to worry about—like becoming sexually self-possessed and empowered and doing our best to adhere to a relational ethic that includes honoring the dignity and respect of all people, regardless of sexual and gender identity. Yeah.

How Intersectionality, Privilege, and Power Play Out in Our World

Did you know that gender stereotypes about girls and boys can extend to issues like who has the right to do a certain job and who doesn't, and who has an aptitude for science and math and who does not? Who gets to be doctors, lawyers, and wear suits to work, and who is destined to stay home and cook, clean, and raise the children (guess who?). That who gets paid more for doing the same type of work can depend on gender? Gender biases (prejudices) in our culture about girls and boys might even influence whether you decide to major in physics or education in college! They can determine who is considered better, smarter, who gets power and respect and who doesn't!

Kind of upsetting, right?

As long as people have existed (which is a very long time), societies, cultures, religions, and legal systems have discriminated against people based on gender (and race, ethnicity, sexual identity, economic status). Generally, in our society, this has meant that (white, heterosexual) men have the power and opportunity and everyone who is not a (white, heterosexual) man is out of luck. Women of all backgrounds and sexual orientations have struggled to gain the right to have a life and work outside of the home.

These struggles are far from over.

This is clear when you hear biased comments from friends, people at school, and even your teachers and coaches and other adults in your life, like:

* *Girls are so emotional, but boys are more rational.*

* OR *Girls care more about relationships than boys do.*

* OR *Boys are better at science and math.*

* OR *There are some sports a girl shouldn't play.*

* OR *Boys' sports are more exciting than girls' sports.* (Sigh. Clearly, people who say stuff like this do not also follow soccer played by the US Women's National Team! Megan Rapinoe! Duh!)

Biases about what men and boys can and should aspire to do versus what women and girls can't and shouldn't are lurking underneath the surface of our society and culture, just like your sheets are hiding underneath your comforter or the basement of your house is hiding under the rest of it.

If you were to draw a diagram of these gender biases they would form a hierarchy that might look something like this:

Male	Rational	Political/Public	Soul	Strong	Independent	Leader
Female	Emotional	Domestic/Private	Body	Weak	Dependent/Relational	Supporter

We've been conditioned to associate men and boys with being rational, political, independent, with soul, with strength, with leadership. We *privilege* those traits that are above the line as more worthy, more important, more powerful, as better and more valuable traits to possess.

We associate women and girls with the "lesser" traits that fall underneath that line, traits that we consider less privileged and powerful and worthwhile. We tend to *devalue* the traits that we associate as feminine and with women and girls.

Because of the biological sex we were assigned at birth, girls and boys grow up gendered, and they are *gendered into* these traits and this hierarchy, too.

We raise boys and young men to be confident, rational, independent leaders in their professions and the public sphere, yet we convince girls and women that they are more emotional, caregiving beings, better destined and designed for motherhood and raising children.

Times have changed, but these beliefs about men and women are still around.

You face these biases even if it doesn't feel like they're there. Trust me—they are. There will come a day when you will contend with them if you haven't already. When you do, I want you to be prepared, alert, and ready to unpack them—so you can resist them.

Now let's talk about intersectionality.

If you identify as a girl and you are also Black, Latina, or any race other than white, you face a double whammy of bias: about gender *and* your racial background. If you are a Latino man who's gay, you face that double whammy, too: about your racial background and your sexual identity. Or you might face a *triple* whammy of bias if you are a lesbian Chinese woman, as you grow up and go out into the working world. (That's what *intersectionality* is about.)

I know. This isn't fair.

Hierarchies based on male and female are complicated by race, ethnicity, sexual orientation, economic background, and religion, not to mention your status as a citizen versus an immigrant (the list goes on). These identities help determine your value—or *nonvalue*—in our society.

These hierarchies also teach us *which bodies* are more valuable than other bodies. For example, they teach us that white, male, heterosexual bodies are the most valuable bodies, more valuable than all Black bodies, even if they are male, and all Latino bodies, and all gay bodies. They teach us that all male bodies are more valuable than all women's bodies (whether Black, Latina, Asian, etc.), and all male and female bodies are more valuable than transgender bodies, period.

Ugh. Ugh, ugh, *ugh*.

Gender activists, teachers, and scholars have been trying to dismantle these hierarchies and biases as if they are some gigantic Lego sculptures that have taken over the living room. These people (myself included) want to take them down brick by tiny brick, until they are completely gone and there are no bumpy Legos left to hurt the soft undersides of our feet.

Because hurt us these hierarchies do—they hurt *all* of us, including those of us who are born lucky enough to sit at the top of the pyramid.

It is tough, painstaking work, but without it, people lack opportunities, hope, fair futures, and so many other things, including respect, the right to be valued as a human being among all others, the right to love who we want, and the right to live free from violence against their person, including sexual violence.

I know. Super important.

Maybe something *you* want to become an activist about, too.

What Pronouns Do You Favor?

So, which pronouns do other people use when they refer to you?

He, him, his?

She, her, hers?

It's likely that it is one *or* the other.

But *maybe*, just maybe, people use *they, them, theirs* to refer to you. Or another set, or combination, of preferred pronouns.

Notice how I asked that first question—what pronouns do *other people* use to refer to you?

This is because most of us (so far) grow up into a gender usually determined by our biological sex assigned at birth, and people assign pronouns based on that biological sex. Depending on your sex at birth and those pronouns people and language automatically assigned to you, *you* became *gendered* as either masculine or feminine, whether you like it or not, and whether it suits you or not.

And speaking of *you*:

If you could choose your own pronouns (which you could! You can!), would you keep the ones that you were assigned at birth? Or are you interested in changing your pronouns?

If so, why? And if not, why not?

And if you aren't sure—no big deal, either.

How *you gender yourself* isn't a decision you need to make today, and it's also something you can play around with at different points in your life. It's also not a decision you need to make at all! Some people are totally comfortable with the way the world genders them at birth and feel happy in that skin. Which is great, if that works for you.

But if you don't feel good about the way people have gendered you, know that you have the right to ask people to use different pronouns.

Whether you want to stick with those pronouns or try on some new ones, we all have some critical thinking to do about gender. Once we understand how the world shapes us, there is a much greater chance that we can become empowered around our gender identity, regardless of which gender fits us best. Contemplating gender is for everyone. Only then will we be able to dismantle those hierarchies that tell us who and how we can be and should not be (based on whether we happen to have a vagina or a penis! I mean, really?!?!).

Questioning Gender:

Make a list of all the ways you've been stereotypically gendered in your life. Start by looking around your bedroom. Is it decorated in a way that shouts "boy" or "girl"—in its colors, the kinds of things you hang on your walls, etc.? How does the way you dress reflect— or challenge—the way you've been gendered? What about your activities and the things you are encouraged to study and do at school? The sports you play (or don't)?

Spend some time reflecting on ways that being gendered has *empowered* you. But also spend some time thinking about ways that being gendered may have *disempowered* you. Have you ever been told that girls don't do science or math? Or that girls should care about relationships more than other things? Have you been told that boys should be tough and play sports, not do theater or ballet? Does the way you've been gendered feel right to you? If so, reflect on why and how. If not, take some time to think about what doesn't feel right, and what steps you might begin to take to change this.

Now, if you are daring enough, sit down with one of your parents (or both!) and ask them how gender influenced the way they raised you. Have they thought about this? (My guess is, probably yes. If not, then you can help point it out to them!)

What Does It Mean to Be a Boy, a Guy, a Man?*

Guys Have Feelings, Too: Moving Beyond Stereotypes

Guys are champion performers.

They should receive Oscars for Best Actor (in general), Best Asshole (yup!), Best Pretender at Emotionless Invulnerability. I could think of a dozen different roles that guys typically play on college campuses (and before and beyond), in their effort to,

---

* If you're reading this right now and you don't identify as a boy, a guy, a man, you might be wondering, what does all of this mean for me? Read on, though, because it's relevant for you! It's relevant for all of us, because at some point in our lives, we experience gender stereotypes in some shape or form, because that is how the world categorizes itself, even if that's not how we identify.

well, perform *guyness*. I learned this when I started doing my research about sex.

But before I talked to them, I assumed that college men would tell me something like the following:

* ✳ Casual sex and hooking up are the best ever.

* ✳ They love not having to care about their partners.

* ✳ They have no interest in loving or being loved.

* ✳ They have no interest in a committed relationship.

* ✳ Guys are invulnerable and immune to feeling.

* ✳ When it comes to sex and relationships, they're basically all jerks.

* ✳ If you dissent from any of the above, then you're not considered a "real guy."

I wasn't alone in these assumptions. The women I interviewed also assumed these things about guys. Many people assume these things about guys, and that displaying such qualities is how a heterosexual guy proves his heterosexuality.

What's more, boys in our culture are raised to believe that all men are basically sexual predators. That all men want to do and all they think about is having sex with any and all women (because we also assume all guys are heterosexual). That if they aren't like this, then something must be wrong with them.

But when I talked with guys in private, they told me a

completely different story about themselves that explodes these stereotypes.

Their message?

Guys care *a lot*. They long to be loved. They'd like to have emotionally connective, meaningful sex. Hookup culture (more on that later) isn't that great, even though they know they're supposed to think it's amazing. Guys are not jerks. They're not all sexual predators, either. They're actually really nice, good people. They get hurt and get their hearts broken like everybody else. And they don't like the fact that the proving ground for guys seems to be to act like assholes.

But . . .

They feel they have to pretend that the above is *not* the truth. That guys are required to act like someone they aren't. They do this for women, sure, but even more so, they do this to prove themselves to *other guys*.

Hence the Oscars of Guyness.

Growing up into manhood and masculinity in our culture seems to involve getting really good at hiding who you are, especially in front of other men. Other men hold the power of deciding that you are not one of them—that you're not a real man—so you've got to get good at performing stereotypical guyness so you can pass the real-man test.

But hiding who you are is *not* good. It isolates you. It cuts you off from relationships and talking to the people you need. It silences you and makes you feel alone. It prevents you from fulfilling your real desires, and sometimes even from figuring out what your real desires are.

So What If You Identify as a Gay Guy? Does That Change Expectations?

Yes and no.

We tend to throw all boys into the same heterosexual pot because (if you recall from the chapter on sexual identity) we live in a heterosexist world. We assume that all boys are heterosexual until proven otherwise, which *also* means that all boys, gay or straight, learn to "perform guyness." Until a guy comes out as gay, bi, trans, they face the same performance issues as everyone else—and likely afterward, too.

Our culture also teaches that for boys who openly show their emotions—if they cry, if they show enthusiasm (and not just because they scored a touchdown), if they are heartfelt, vulnerable people—that this is a sign they are gay.

Translation?

Caring + Seeking love + Love + Excitement + Sadness ≠ Heterosexual Guy.

Even more terrible, we teach that acting "gay" in this way is bad.

Our culture associates caring, loving, vulnerability, and emotion with women and femininity. This also means these things are devalued. As soon as a boy or a man displays qualities associated with women, he gets demoted to the same status as a woman or girl, he gets labeled "feminine." (What's one of the worst insults a guy can get in gym class or on their sports team? Answer: You run like a girl. You play like a girl. Right?) The message society has for gay, bi, and certainly trans men (at least for now) is that they are "lesser men" because they supposedly act more like women and display womanly qualities. This is where intersectionality comes in again, and why being, say, Latinx and a gay man is a double, devaluing whammy in our culture. Not to mention what this means for our view of women. Grrrrr.

(I know, I know! Our society really sucks sometimes!)

This is also why if a star football or basketball player (sports we associate with super-manly men) comes out as gay it explodes people's brains. And why it's been so difficult for male pro athletes to go public about being gay (see Jason Collins, the former NBA player, for example). We have this block on the idea that gay men can also be "manly men." Gay men face a whole host of stereotypes about who they are supposed to be and not be, too, once they are out. (They are *not* supposed to be quarterbacks, right? They are *only* supposed to be theater types!) And like hetero men, they face their own set of boxes they are supposed to fit themselves into like house cats.

What I hope *you* are asking as you read, is this:

Really?! REALLY?!

Why does our culture *do* these things and teach us these messed-up values? Why can't all guys just, well, be who they really are, whoever that happens to be? What's so bad about being womanly and feminine anyway? Why does our society devalue such wonderful things like openheartedness and emotion and the desire to love and be loved? And why in the world is the cost of being a man so freaking high?

Why Do We Fail Boys and Men So Badly?

If what I've learned in my research is true—that who guys say they are is not who we think they are, and that they are as diverse as can be in every way imaginable—then we've gotten guys very wrong. The hierarchies that privilege certain qualities and opportunities for (white, heterosexual) men are actually the very same things that make so many men feel alienated from themselves.

But if this is also true, then why do so many young men go along with stereotypes if they aren't really *real*? Why do they play the role of the unfeeling guy if they feel things as deeply as they claim?

Fear is one big reason. Going against the norms of culture and society is a risk. Guys are scared of people questioning their masculinity and deciding that they're not "real guys." Guys worry about losing their friends. Guys worry about the cost of showing too much emotion. Guys worry that if they don't prove themselves as real guys, then no one will want to be in a relationship with them, friendly or romantic. That they'll get thrown into the reject pile.

The cost of these fears—and of us getting guys so wrong—is enormous.

We are teaching boys to hide who they really are, in order for them to be considered real men. We are teaching boys to show people they don't need to be loved or to love others, that they are emotionless, hardened, invulnerable creatures. We are teaching boys that to be sensitive, vulnerable, and caring is bad—that real men aren't like this.

The cost of this isn't paid only by the guys. Everyone has to deal with the repercussions of men having to tamp down their emotions and to act in ways that are not true to themselves. One of the biggest costs of so much hiding and acting as someone other than one's true self is with respect to sex and consent.

The Problem of Stereotypical Masculinity for Sex and Consent

Remember how I said that to be a "real guy" is to act like a sexual predator? To pretend you don't care about sex or your partners?

Just think about what this might mean for a guy's attitude toward consent.

Our culture raises boys and young men to *push* for sex—to push girls for sex, specifically. Guys learn that they should always push a girl as far as she is willing to go, and farther than that, ideally. Our culture teaches guys they should always be out for themselves when it comes to sex—sex is about *their* orgasms and nobody else's. That it's normal for a guy to be selfish in sexual situations, to "take" rather than to "give," and normal for a girl to "give" rather than "take." (Who cares about *her*? This is all about *me*.) Girls are to be *used* for sex. Guys are not supposed to respect their partners—a girl is a means to an orgasm, nothing more.

Guys are supposed to care about conquests, not connections, about "having sex like a man," which translates into sleeping with someone, then walking away like they don't care about the sex or their partner. Guys are supposed to be "players," which translates to having sex with as many women as possible, without developing feelings for any of them.

People have all kinds of biases about gay men and gay sex, too. Some people assume that the only thing two men would want from each other is sex and more sex, and the more anonymous the sex, the better. The default assumption is that men want sex without emotion so two men are in luck and can have as much emotionless, noncommittal sex as they want. Or, people assume that two gay men together is akin to two women. Or, people assume that one man in the couple will act the "man's role" in sex and become the person who pushes and pushes past their partner's boundaries and uses their partner for orgasms (i.e., be the taker), while the other person's role is to act "the woman" (i.e., be the giver).

But having sex according to societal stereotypes and expectations does not tend to fulfill guys, regardless of their sexual orientation. Guys are diverse, and performing in these inauthentic, stereotypical ways keeps them away from the relationships and love they long for.

Socializing boys and men in this way also socializes them *against consent* as a value. Think about it. Consent, at a basic level, is about respecting someone's boundaries, their wishes and desires; it's about respecting them as partners. Yet if guys are socialized to *push* their partners—to push and push and not take *no* for an answer—to *not respect* their partners *and* to *use* their partners like objects . . .

Well, this is not a recipe for consent.

And this is not good for anyone. But it's especially not good for girls and women who are most often the victims of sexual violence.

So What's a Boy to Do?

This entire book is designed to help you to ask questions about yourself—questions that lead you to thinking about what sex and consent mean to you. It's designed to help you realize and practice your relational ethic and values as you journey through life.

Figuring out who you are as a boy or a man—if this is how you identify—is a big part of this journey. I want you to figure out what masculinity and being a boy, a man, a guy means to *you*. Whether you are hetero, gay, bi, trans or cis, I want you to become the person you really are. I *don't* want you to act out a bunch of cultural stereotypes that are not your own and that make you feel *not you*. I also don't want you to become a victim to all of the shoulds and have-tos and gottas of being a "real guy" (which you know by now is all a big performance anyway). Many young men are caught between how they're supposed to act and how they wish they could authentically act.

Defying cultural stereotypes, especially the kind I'm describing, is not easy. It takes a lot of confidence and a lot of work. That's why we're here, though. We're here to work, to think, to wonder, and to gain some self-knowledge. If you do identify as a boy, it's imperative that you engage in this difficult work of thinking about what masculinity means to you. The cost is too high if you don't—to you and to all your current and future relationships.

Now It's Your Turn:

1. Regardless of how you identify, make a list of as many traits as you've learned to associate with being a boy, a guy, a man. It might be personality qualities, it might be behaviors and things boys and men are expected to do. (For example, "boys don't cry" is a classic lesson that so many boys are still taught.)

1A. Now, if you do identify as a boy, compare those qualities to what you really know about yourself—who you believe you really are. Which qualities fit you well, and which ones do not? Do you find yourself performing some of these stereotypes, for fear of looking stupid in front of others, or fear of being rejected? (It's okay if the answer is yes—we all do this kind of thing.) Do any of the things on this list conflict with your relational ethic? If so, why? How so?

1B. Now make a list of people you feel safe with. Men, women, boys, girls, folks who identify otherwise. Anyone you can think of. Pick one person on this list, and think about whether you can be yourself with that person, and maybe even have a conversation with them about some of the stereotypes you've learned to inhabit, yet that don't make you feel good when you act this way.

2. Name a man you really respect, and try to think of what about this person makes you respect him. Think of as many reasons as you can. Are there any ways that he defies cultural stereotypes about boys and men with how he acts, what he looks like, what he does?

3. Ask some girls and women in your life what they've learned about what boys/guys are like. Ask them if they have any ideas about what they wish boys were allowed to be like. (Maybe even ask your mom!)

4. Open a page in your journal and describe what you think your "ideal man" is like. Don't worry—write whatever you want, even if you wouldn't say it out loud to someone else. This is your journal and no one is looking.

What Does It Mean to Be a Girl, a Woman?*

Let's Get Those Stereotypes Out on the Table

Sweet. Kind. Friendly. Emotional. Agreeable. Patient. Support-ive. Nurturing.

This list of qualities sounds positive, right? But these quali-ties also can amount to not-so-positive characteristics like *passive*, as in, not so assertive.

---

* Again, if you're reading this right now and you don't identify as a girl, a woman, you might be wondering, what does all of this mean for me? Read on, though, because it's relevant for you! It's relevant for all of us, because at some point in our lives, we experience gender stereotypes in some shape or form, because that is how the world categorizes itself, even if that's not how we identify.

Traditionally, girls and women have been raised to nod their heads, smile, be supportive, take care of the men in their lives, in whatever role that was (daughter, mother, wife). Today, girls and women aren't expected to act in quite the same way as in the 1950s, but people still expect similar personality traits of girls and women. Maybe you are nodding your head as you read because you know *exactly* what I am talking about, because you've been raised to be these things, too.

There is nothing wrong with being sweet, kind, patient.

But . . .

When these qualities become the expectations with which *all* girls and women must comply—when girls and women must *perform* these traits or they are not considered feminine or womanly enough—these traits become burdens stopping girls and women from becoming who they really are.

In the 1990s, feminist psychologists Lyn Mikel Brown and Carol Gilligan published the book *Meeting at the Crossroads: Women's Psychology and Girls' Development.* It was important research for many reasons, but especially for one *big* finding: the book explored how girls and boys are raised differently. Brown and Gilligan found that around the age of twelve boys expand and girls contract. And they weren't talking about people's bodies.

They were talking about outlooks and possibilities. Boys in our culture are raised to see themselves going out and taking over the world! Of doing anything! Of becoming astronauts and presidents and sports stars and doctors and lawyers! But around the age of twelve, girls' worlds suddenly get very small because girls are expected to care about relationships above all else, focusing on caregiving, being supportive of everyone around them, and deferring to the needs of others over their own.

I know what you're thinking: The 1990s is, like, *ages* ago.

Yes. And times have changed a lot. But these stereotypes persist in the ways we raise boys and. girls. More recently, Lyn Mikel Brown and another feminist psychologist, Sharon Lamb, looked at how consumer culture (Think Disney Princesses! Think Boy Superheroes!) has stepped in to shape boys and girls in ways that reinforce those old stereotypes. The dividing line between how we expect boys to be and act and how we expect girls to be and act is still, well, divided, and Lamb and Brown discuss the many negative stereotypes that people have about girls and women today—stereotypes you have likely already run into, especially if you happen to be a girl. Do any of these sound familiar?

Girls and women are gossips.

They love drama.

They're vapid and vacuous and are obsessed with how they look.

They shop, they put on makeup, they obsess about boys.

They stab people in the back.

They're obsessed with social media because of all the above and because they're vain.

Also, girls and women are slutty.

Consumer culture reinforces these ideas, by selling—and selling hard—these stereotypes through the things girls are encouraged to buy.

These are the not-so-nice counterparts to that first list I gave you (sweet, kind, supportive—that is, passive).

And then:

What about the girls and women who display more stereotypically masculine attributes like assertiveness, authority, power, strength? The girls and women who go after what they want without apology, who are competitive, who rise to positions of great authority? Girls and women who aren't afraid to speak the truth, who aren't trying to be agreeable and super nice all the time?

How does our culture teach us to view *those* kinds of girls and women?

As bitches. Right?

Boys and men can get away with being assertive, confident, with holding someone accountable, with going after promotions, or being captain on a sports team—but girls and women cannot (or they have a much harder time doing this). Girls and women who defy feminine stereotypes and display attributes stereotypically associated with boys and men usually get punished. We reward such girls and women by calling them *bitches* and *bitchy*.

Maybe you are nodding your head again. Maybe you know exactly what I am talking about because either A) you've been called a bitch yourself for these reasons, or B) you've engaged in the bitch-calling of others for these reasons. (Admitting it is the first step to fixing it.)

Another thing that girls and women sometimes get labeled, for dressing in stereotypically masculine ways, for cultivating a stereotypically masculine look and hairstyle, or for being particularly athletic and strong in their bodies?

Lesbians.

Yup! Another thing we Americans can be proud to have cultivated in our society. We choose to denigrate achieving, successful, assertive, athletic, strong women by taking an entire category of women (girls and women who identify as lesbians) and using that identity as a derogatory term for an entire category of girls and women.

Awesome, huh?

There are so many double standards operating here for women and girls that I am dizzy with them.

To sum up: Our society tends to treat (and therefore teach them that) girls and women who display what are typically viewed as positive attributes for men (assertiveness, confidence, go-getter-ness) as problematic and negative and deserving of name-calling and punishment. This is another reason why stereotypes are problematic for all of us. They aren't fair to boys and men, but they are especially not fair to those of us who identify on the girl side of things.

What Does All This Mean for Lesbians, Anyway?

Geez. Well. It's complicated. (Of course, of course!)

We live in a culture where calling a boy "gay" or calling a girl a "lesbian" is a method for insulting someone and telling them that they aren't "measuring up" as a real guy or real girl. Blech.

Just as with the assumptions people make about gay boys and men as stereotypically feminine, people assume that lesbians exhibit stereotypically masculine traits in the ways they dress, style their hair, and in their interests, too (like with sports or hobbies or the colors they prefer to wear).

Of course, we already know that girls and women who display as stereotypically masculine regardless of their sexual identity are not about to be rewarded for displaying these traits. They get punished for it. Unlike gay men who get demoted to the status of women, it's not as if women—lesbian or otherwise—who cross those stereotypes get *promoted* to the status of men. All women get stuck on the bottom half of that privilege hierarchy—being a girl or a woman—in pretty much a permanent and perpetual demotion. So if you identify as a (white) lesbian, you get *doubly* demoted. If you are not white *and* a lesbian, you get *triply* demoted. (This is where we need to think about intersectionality again.)

Yeah, yeah, *yeah.* I know. Ridiculous.

You might be wondering again: Why in the world does our culture always do this stuff? Why do we try to categorize people and cram them into boxes when they are not house cats who *want* to be crammed into boxes? Why do we insist on denigrating people so much? Why can't we just be who we are, however that may be, regardless of our sexual identity? Why, why, *why*?! It isn't fair, it isn't fair!

It really isn't. I'm not gonna lie.

But, but, *but*:

That doesn't mean it has to be this way forever. We can change things. We are changing things. You can be a part of that change. Maybe you are already.

Are You a Feminist? Womanist? Mujerista?

Back when I was eighteen, I used to say to people, "I'm not a feminist!" I said it all the time. (I am shuddering right now as I admit this to you.)

I can't believe there was a day in my life when I thought this was true. But it's because I had feminism all wrong. Feminism has long had a PR (public relations) problem, which is a big reason why I dissociated myself from it. It's not the feminists' fault, either! People in our culture who don't like feminism and feminists, who may even hate feminism and feminists—i.e. misogynists—people who are *afraid* of the empowering things feminism can do for girls and women and really for all of us, have sold a story full of destructive lies about feminism.

Here are just a few of those lies: Feminists aren't feminine, they dress like men, don't like men, don't care about how they look, are always angry, are against romance, and so on and so forth.

The thing is, back when I was a young woman, I bought all of this and decided I couldn't be a feminist because:

* I really love to wear dresses and heels.

* I love to read about fashion.

* I like boys—a lot.

* I have long hair and wear makeup.

✳ I love the color pink (and purple for that matter).

✳ I love romance, love, relationships, all that stuff.

I know. I sound super girlie in a way that might make Sharon Lamb and Lyn Mikel Brown cringe. (I also want to be clear: I don't think there's anything wrong with short hair or not wearing makeup or liking girls instead of boys or disliking the color pink! That isn't the issue.) The problem is that I learned to disassociate anything to do with stereotypical femininity from feminism. And because I am a girlie girl, I thought this meant I couldn't be a feminist.

But so what if I'm girlie? Does that really mean I can't be a feminist?

Maybe *you* have similar feelings and have learned to say *you* aren't a feminist because of similar reasons—whether you are a boy or a girl reading this.

Big mistake!

Feminism has *nothing* to do with how you dress or if you love the color pink or if you love to love and be loved and wish some nice boy would send you flowers (or some nice girl for that matter) and/or ask you on a date. Feminism has *nothing* to do with the negative, superficial things that people afraid of feminism sell about feminists.

And newsflash:

You are a feminist.
Or a *womanist* (that's Black feminism).
Or a *mujerista* (that's Latinx feminism).

Boy or girl or someone outside of the gender binary or whether the jury is out on your gender and/or your sexuality, you *are* a feminist. I know you are even if *you* don't know that you are yet.

What Feminism Is: Getting Beyond the Lies

Feminism is why women have the right to vote, why girls grow up to play sports if they want to, why girls and women have equal access to an education, to jobs, to all the different kinds of opportunities that white men have had since the beginning of time just because they are white men.

Feminism is also a state of mind, one that is essential when it comes to thinking about who you are (there's that self-knowledge business again), and also about sex and consent (of course). At its most basic, foundational level, feminism is about the following:

Voice.
Choice.
Opportunity/Access.
Justice for all.

Whatever name you claim for it, feminism is grounded in your ability and your right to speak and be heard on behalf of your own experience. Feminism is about feeling like you have *real* options: that there are many paths and possibilities ahead of you and it is up to you which one you pick. Feminism is about access for everybody to the various corners and spaces in the public sphere. Feminism is about who gets to do what profession and everyone having a fair chance of doing the jobs they'd like to do. Feminism cares about justice and dignity for all people regardless of sexual or gender identity. Feminism demands respect for you and for all people.

Feminism challenges *patriarchy*.

Patriarchy is a system or social order that favors men and masculinity above all else, and where heterosexual men are the privileged class within patriarchy. It places heterosexual men at the top of the pyramid and as destined to be, born to be, in charge of all things. We still live within a patriarchal society, culture, and government, and pretty much all religions are patriarchal institutions. We are basically, all of us, swimming in patriarchy, all the time. In fact, patriarchy and patriarchal institutions are the authors behind all the problematic stereotypes about boys, men, girls, and women we've been discussing, that everyone is working so hard to perform, and which force so many of us to hide who we really are.

Feminism and its varieties do not propose replacing patriarchy with matriarchy (a system where hierarchies would be flipped and women would dominate men). Feminism favors egalitarian systems where all people—whether women or men—trans or cis—or folks outside the gender binary, and regardless of sexual identity, race, ethnicity, educational background—have equal opportunity and access.

Feminism is about *not* performing roles and scripts that have been handed down like laws to you, especially if they make you feel bad about yourself. Feminism *is* about your ability to take those roles and scripts you inherit and look at them, decide what you think about them, and throw them off if you don't like them and want to go a different direction. Feminism also encourages you to rewrite those roles and scripts and stereotypes and expectations so that they better fit the person you are, better express your desires, and better honor the goal of respect and dignity for all people.

Feminism *empowers* us—all of us—to make *real* choices. To navigate cultural, societal, and religious attitudes and expectations with self-knowledge, an understanding of our own needs and desires; a critical, analytical eye about biases around gender; and an eye toward justice for all people, regardless of sexual, gender, and racial identity.

Remember the diagram in the chapter on gender? The one that privileges the traits associated with men and masculinity (rational, strong, individual, public, etc.) and puts the traits associated with femininity and women on the bottom half (the disempowered half) of it? And how I said that if a boy or man comes out as gay he suddenly gets demoted to the level of women and associated with the stereotypical traits of femininity? And how intersectionality reckons with the multiple levels of demotion that certain members of our society deal with depending on how their race and sexual identity intersect? The double, triple, even quadruple demotions some members of our communities might face?

Well, feminism does its best to *shatter* these hierarchies that promote and demote us based on personality traits and the bodies we were born with and things like sexual orientation and race and disability. Feminism does its best to *explode* these hierarchies—between men and women, the rational and the emotional, the individual and the relational, the public and the private—because most people are not one thing *or* the other, but are a mixture of both, and because *all* these traits are positive when they work in conjunction with one another. To be only one thing (rational) and not the other (emotional) is simply not good for us. To believe that how we identify means we are not allowed to embody certain traits is as disempowering and problematic as it gets. To believe that because we are gay or bi or lesbian or transgender we can't be an NFL football player or we can't wear long, flowing dresses or we can't, we can't, *we just can't be ourselves* is just plain awful and unjust.

Feminism, in its true form, has nothing to do with man-hating and pink-hating. It doesn't determine who wears lipstick and who is angry and who is sweet.

Feminism is about *real* empowerment.

We all need feminism, womanism, mujerista theology. Women, men, girls, boys, nonbinary people, and transgender people. All of us.

Sluts, Prudes, and Victim-Blaming

Now I really have your attention, don't I!

I've spoken before about name-calling, but I want to come back to it. Girls and women suffer an inordinate amount of name-calling during their lives, often from other girls and women. It's one of those toxic things our often-toxic culture encourages of women, by women, and between women. We pit women and girls against one another, especially when it comes to areas of life related to sex, the body, and the way women and girls are objectified and judged with respect to sex.

Maybe the word *slut* resonates particularly harshly with you.

Or maybe the word *prude* does instead.

Or maybe, so far, you've lived unscathed by these labels (lucky you!).

Or maybe *you* have applied these labels to people at your school, or even people you call your friends. Maybe you've done this as an act of self-preservation and as a defense mechanism— so you could avoid this kind of negative labeling yourself. Or because you were in the middle of a group of people you thought you could impress by name-calling. And because sometimes name-calling makes us feel powerful for at least a minute and feeling powerful is often in short supply if you are a girl.

Either way, girls and women suffer a lot of name-calling during their lives, whereas boys and men tend to get the positive kinds of labels that make other men give them high fives. Not fair, I know.

Now is the time to pull out your relational ethic again.

My guess? If you're honest, you already know beyond a shadow of a doubt that name-calling is not acting like a good friend. That labels stick, and when they do, they can have ruinous social and relational consequences for their targets.

Name-calling is *never* good.

It's one of those toxic things we do to each other—that *all* of us do to each other at some point in our childhoods and in our young adulthoods and in our adulthoods, too. It contradicts everything good about our humanity, about sex, about being empowered with respect to gender, sex, and consent. And when it happens to women and girls? It puts all women and girls in an impossible situation with respect to sex.

Girls are raised to be virginal (prudes!), yet girls are also expected to have sex and be casual about it (sluts!). Somehow, girls and women are supposed to be *both* virginal *and* casual about sex. Impossible, I know.

This unfair burden that girls and women carry—to walk the impossible line of being virginal while at the same time having lots of sex and being super-sexy—translates to other problems. It places the burden of saying *no* to sex on women. In the previous chapter, when I spoke of how boys are raised to push for more and more sex, and to even push past women's nos? Well, women are raised to believe that if they *don't say no and don't say no forcefully enough*, they are implicitly agreeing to whatever a guy pushes for.

We are going to come back to this topic in the section on consent, but I wanted to make this link *here* before we get *there*: that women and girls tend to shoulder the blame for the sexual violence enacted on them.

Why didn't you say no?

Why didn't you fight the guy off?

Why did you let him do that to you?

You must have given him the wrong idea! You shouldn't go around acting like such a slut, then guys wouldn't try to have sex with you! You know you wanted it! That's what you get!

This is called victim-blaming. And it's not okay. It's not fair to girls and women. It's not right. It's very, very wrong.

I want you to think on this and sit with it: the *fact* that for ages and ages girls and women have been taught that it *is* their responsibility to prevent sexual violence. That it's our responsibility to *not get raped* by not walking alone, by not going to frat parties, by not drinking too much, by not wearing short skirts, by not doing all sorts of things. And when we *do* do all these things, the finger often gets pointed at us for somehow not preventing a man from ignoring our no's. It becomes *our fault* that we got raped by the frat boy because we went to the frat party in the first place and we wore a sexy dress while we were there.

We need to face this unfair, unjust reality together—so we can transform it. All of us do, whether we identify as girls or not.

Some Reflections for the Road:

1. Make a list of as many traits you've learned to associate with being a girl, a woman. It might be personality qualities, it might be behaviors and things girls and women are expected to do. (For example: Girls are babies. Girls are drama queens.)

1A. Now compare those qualities to what you really know about yourself—who you believe you really are. Which qualities fit you well, and which ones do not? Do you find yourself performing some of these stereotypes, for fear of looking stupid in front of others, or fear of being rejected? (It's okay if the answer is yes—we all do this kind of thing.) Do any of the things on this list, conflict with your relational ethic? If so, why? How so?

1B. Now make a list of people you feel safe with. Men, women, boys, girls, folks who identify otherwise. Anyone you can think of. Pick one person on this list, and think about whether you can be yourself with that person, and maybe even have a conversation with them about some of the stereotypes you've learned to inhabit, yet that don't make you feel good when you act this way.

2. Name a woman you really respect, and try to think of what about this person makes you respect her. Think of as many reasons as you can. Are there any ways that she defies cultural stereotypes about girls and women with how she acts, what she looks like, what she does?

3. Talk to some boys and men in your life (maybe even your dad!). Ask them what they've learned about what girls/women are like. Ask them if they have any ideas about what they wish girls were allowed to be like, or if they wish our culture had different ideas about what it means to be a girl/woman.

4. Answer this question: Are you a feminist? If your impulse is to answer *no*, write down some reasons why you think this is. What did you learn about feminism before reading this book? What do you think about feminism now after reading this chapter?

What Is SEX? Why Does It Matter? What Does It Mean to Be a SEXUAL BEING?

So You're Super Sex-Curious! And That Is Awesome!

What is this sex thing? How does it all work? Am I gonna like it? Who am I gonna have it with? When am I gonna have it?! How does a person figure out all this sex stuff? Who can I talk to about it? Who *can't* I talk to about it? What does it all mean?! How does one learn how to have sex? What happens after kissing?

Can I kiss *you*? Can I kiss *him*? What about *her*?

Is kissing a bunch of people going to help me figure out this stuff?

These are good questions. Normal questions. Questions that show you are *curious.*

Curiosity is *great.*

Curious people ask Big Questions and asking Big Questions is awesome. I want you to feel free to ask any and every question you have about sex and everything related to it. I also want to make sure you have people with whom you can explore these questions and ponderings and wonderings about sex. I don't want you to be alone in your curiosity and questions.

When I was a kid, I got to a point where I was super curious about sex.

Did I ask my parents my questions?

NO WAY! My parents pretty much had a KEEP OUT sign on their door for the sex subject. Sex was not up for discussion in my house. So, what did I do when I had questions?

I secretly read all my mother's romance novels!

When she wasn't around, I would take them down from the shelf and search for all the sexy bits. When I was in the bookstore, I also did this. My friends and I talked about stuff and tried to figure it out on our own, and sometimes an older sibling helped us with the necessary info. We passed around novels like *Forever* by Judy Blume (which my mother forbade me to read, BTW) and *Flowers in the Attic* (not the best resource for sex, given that it's a horror novel about incest, but we read it anyway). Eventually in school we had a week-long, mandatory biology lesson on the technicalities of sex—it was minimal and gave us little more than a tour of the male and female pelvises.

My sex education was not ideal, in other words, and asking

Big Questions about sex was not encouraged. I don't want the same situation for you. And when I *did* start kissing people, I had no idea what to expect or what to do—which was both good and bad (more on this later).

Though this book is not a how-to for sex, a big part of your sex education (in my opinion)—maybe the biggest, most important part—is the one that helps you get to a place where you feel confident and secure enough to ask questions about sex when you have them. To know where your resources are to seek answers, and to know who your conversation partners are for talking through your questions and ideas and opinions about sex.

By the time you make it through this book, I want you to feel okay with where you are in relation to your sexual present, too—whether you've had a little bit of experience in the sexual intimacy department, a lot, or none at all. I want you to feel proud of who you are and where you are in this regard, because becoming a *critical thinker* about sex is something that should make you feel amazing. You are on the road to sexual enlightenment and liberation *and* you are way ahead of people on the sex front, even lots and lots of adults! (There are eighty-year-old people walking around who have *never done any critical thinking about sex*. I *know*. I can't believe they missed out on such an important experience either!)

I want you to do a lot of thinking and wondering and pondering about sex and a lot of getting to know who you are as a sexual being *before* you go about actually experimenting with sexual intimacy (even though experimentation is, eventually, part of that journey, too). Despite popular opinion, sexual liberation is *not* about doing a bunch of sexual things or proving to others you've done a bunch of sexual things ("Yeah, so I did that and this and that with her and him and them"). True sexual liberation is about consciousness, self-awareness, self-possession.

Having Lots of Sex Doesn't Mean You Know Anything About Sex!

I will never forget the conversation I had with a group of students, most of them seniors in college, about the meaning of sex.

I'd just given a lecture to a large group of students, faculty, and staff at this university. Afterward, about twelve students stayed around to chat. It was a casual conversation, with some lingering questions related to my talk.

At one point, a young woman asked, "What's the difference between sex and holding hands, anyway? Like, *why* is sex such a big deal?"

She wasn't kidding. Of course she knew there was a pretty big difference between having sex and holding hands, *technically.* But she was asking a much Bigger Question about why having sex matters. She was asking about the *meaning* of sex.

These students had already had a lot of sex—they'd shared this fact pretty early in our conversation. So, like any annoying professor, I lobbed the question back to the group: "Why *is* sex such a big deal?" The students hemmed and hawed, so I prompted them again:

"Well, what is good sex to you?" I asked. "What does good sex look like?"

This question *really* stumped the group.

"What do you mean, 'good sex'?" one of them asked.

"You know, *good sex!*" I thought my question was self-explanatory. "What are the circumstances that create good sex? Where are you? Are you in a bed, by the ocean, at a party, in a bathroom? Who are you with and what are they like? Are you in a relationship or not in a relationship? Are you in love with the person or does that not matter to you? Is there lots of communication, are there orgasms, does it go on for a long time or a short time? What do you like and not like that makes it good or not good?"

Eventually the students explained the following:

They'd never really thought about good sex before.

No one had ever invited them to consider what good sex might be.

In other words, no one had invited them to become *thinkers* about sex—this thing I want so much for *you*, the reader, to do.

Here I had a bunch of college students who were sexually active and yet they'd never thought about good sex—in large part, because they grew up in a world and within communities and circumstances that never *invited* them to consider this question.

This, to me, is a crime.

Though these college students could claim a lot of sexual experience, *technically*, they were only in the very beginning stages of becoming sexually enlightened, sexually liberated, sexually *empowered*—because *that* requires the kind of knowledge and pondering and wondering that *literally going and having sex* isn't going to give a person, at least not all on its own. Having sex a bunch will give you sexual experience—that is true. But we too often confuse sexual experience with sexual knowledge. These are not one and the same. And having all the sexual experience in the world does not mean that any of this sex was good or that you've come away with a sense of what good sex is to you.

Sexual empowerment requires knowing that you have the *right* and the *responsibility* to ask more than just, "How do I orgasm and how do I give someone else an orgasm?" (Good questions, but these can't be the only ones.)

I want *you* to wonder about good sex and everything it might encompass: the how, the where, the why, the with-whom, the when. I want you to think about what it means to be ready to have sex for the first time—a question that is not easy to answer, especially since I also want you to work hard to shut out all the noise around you telling you when you are *supposed to* feel ready. I want you to give lots of thought to what you want from sex, how you want to have sex (or not!) under what circumstances you think you'd like to have sex and with whom might you like to have it. I want you to think about what it means to be a good partner to someone else—and what someone else being a good partner to you would mean. I want you to read about sex, read about love, read stories both good and not so good that will help you understand sex and relationships better. I want you to wonder about the *meaning* of sex, and under what circumstances might it *become* meaningful to you.

This is a lot to process, but I hope you will wonder and ponder and consider and reconsider all of this like mad as you move through this part of your life. As you get older and gain more life experience, relationship experience, and yes, sexual experience, too, these questions will make more and more sense, and new questions will arise in you, too. You have the right to ask any and all questions, and a responsibility—on your own and on your future partner's behalf—to ask them.

Eventually when you do have sex, I want you to do all that same kind of thinking afterward, all over again. Sex requires us to be thinking beings, and having sex should empower us to keep thinking about sex and what is good and meaningful to us and to our partners (even when it fails to live up to our expectations and hopes, too).

Many Kinds of Sex!

What do we mean when we use the word *sex* anyway? What does it mean to "have sex"?

Are we talking about heterosexual sex? (Sex between a man and a woman? Sex between a woman and a transgender man?)

Gay sex? (Sex between men?)

Lesbian sex? (Sex between women?)

All kinds of sex? (Sex between all kinds of people!)

And when we say sex, do we mean all-things-sexual that are possible? (Oral sex, anal sex, kissing, touching, etc.?) Do we mean only heterosexual intercourse? Do we mean many kinds of intercourse depending on a person's sexual orientation?

Earlier, we discussed the many kinds of sexual identities, and here we are talking about the many kinds of sex that stem from those identities. People will use the word *sex* as a catchall, but it often has different meanings depending on the person using the word.

During my discussions with students over the years, I've run into people who are careful to distinguish what they mean by sex (what sort of sexual activities they are talking about) and which particular sexual orientation they are evoking in that moment (whether it's lesbian, gay, or heterosexual sex, or another kind). I've also run into many students who, when they talk about sex, really mean heterosexual intercourse, and (even if they've had lots of oral sex, anal sex, and engaged in other acts of sexual intimacy) that if they haven't yet had heterosexual intercourse, then they can still claim virginity. (They are hetero-sexist about it and are invested in being so.)

But lately, more and more people understand virginity and having sex in relation to sexual identity—that if you are hetero-sexual, then heterosexual intercourse counts as first-time sex; if you are lesbian, then oral sex determines this; if you are a gay man, then it's anal sex. If you are bi or transgender, then it's whatever genital-to-genital sex you have first that counts.

What I hope is that when *you* talk about sex, that you are not heterosexist about it. I'd like you to become conscious and respectful about the fact that all people are not heterosexual, so when you are discussing sex, you will be sensitive to this.

The Problems with Our Ideas About Virginity

Speaking of virginity.

Maybe you have been raised to be obsessed with virginity, with being a virgin, with "losing" your virginity (or *not* losing it). The older you get, the more you might worry about getting first-time sex over with, or the opposite—hanging on to your virginity even if you are doing all sorts of other sexual things. This preoccupation might be due to your family's religious affiliation or simply because you have grown up in a society that is unhealthily focused on virginity in relation to young adults and gender in particular.

Every now and then, a study comes out about how, even though certain young adults have had oral and/or anal sex twenty-five times (they've done/had "everything but" sex, according to them), they still count themselves virgins. Girls, especially, will count themselves virgins even if they are sexually active in other ways. This is because virginity is not just a religious obsession but also a cultural one (especially if you are a hetero woman). We've turned virginity into a kind of status, something that people (girls and women in particular) can barter with ("I'll give you my V card if you do x, y, or z"). Virginity can make a person feel worthwhile—or not. It can be the determining factor between feeling "trashy" or "slutty" and feeling worthy and valuable.

There is *nothing* wrong with caring about first-time sex. It's good to care about sex, about who you have it with, about doing what you can to ensure that sexual activity is a positive experience for all involved. Concern about virginity—as a label, as a category—can help convey that having sex for the first time should be taken seriously, which it absolutely should!

Religiously devout kids tend to grow up to believe that being a virgin and staying a virgin is essential until they get married. This expectation can be empowering and life-giving for some people, and some young adults talk of how wonderful it was for them to "save sex for marriage" and to only have it with their future, lifetime partners. But for many devout young adults, this attitude turns first-time sex (and any sexual activity) into an unhealthy obsession and the expectations around virginity become soul-crushing.

"Idolizing" virginity can have the effect of turning any sexual activity that occurs outside of marriage into something terrible, sinful, and regrettable. The judging of young adults who engage in sexual activity outside of marriage tends to be very harsh *and* this judging tends to be very gendered. Men can get away with more than women. (And again, all this talk about virginity and sex usually presumes heterosexuality.) Young women are sometimes told that if they dare have sex outside of marriage, they will never find a man willing to marry them later on, that they are irreparably "damaged," because their worth and value depends on their virgin status. The cost of becoming sexually active for so many religious young adults is often high. Women especially worry about losing everything—the respect of their families, religious communities, and even their relationship with God.

Nonreligious and less devout kids tend to grow up divided on first-time sex and virginity. Boys especially grow up with the notion that virginity is something to be gotten rid of, and that remaining a virgin somehow makes them "less masculine." But girls and women also inherit the idea that, starting by the end of high school and certainly during college, they should get rid of their virginity. This attitude teaches people that *not* being sexually active is a problem, that it is shameful. It diminishes the value of sex and the value of the first person you have sex with. This attitude encourages someone to see their partner as an object, as a means to an end, a body to be used. Anytime the worth of one's partner is diminished, care about consent diminishes, too.

Even if you are not raised in a religiously devout household, you may inherit the belief that first-time sex is an extremely big deal and that it should be "with the right person" and happen in romantic-sounding circumstances. And like I said before, taking first-time sex seriously is *good*.

But *idolizing* first-time sex is problematic. It sends an *indirect* message to everyone: that while first-time sex is really important, all the sex that follows is not, that it has little to no value at all.

Because of the ways that we idolize virginity and first-time sex, if someone's first sexual experience does not live up to the cultural myths around it, that person will sometimes describe a sense of *failure* in relation to first-time sex, which encourages that person to devalue all other sexual experiences. They failed to have the "magical first time," so what does it matter if they keep having more unfulfilling sex? What's the impetus to stop having sex, even if it isn't good? The only partner who *really* mattered was the first one, so subsequent partners don't really matter at all.

Let's Decide to Care About All Sex, Not Just First-Time Sex

I don't want this experience for you or for your partners.

What I want for *you* is to even things out. I want you to take *all* sex seriously because *all* sex should matter. I want you to care about your first, second, third, fourth, and fifth times having sex, and so on and so forth, just like I want you to care about your first, second, and third partners (and so on and so forth). I want you to value all the sex you have and all the partners you have it with. I want you to respect sex in general and respect your partners in general, no matter how much or how little sex you've had, and how many or how few partners you've had it with.

Something important to understand: Respecting all sex and all partners, valuing all sex and all partners, isn't a guarantee of good sex. Sometimes the sex people have isn't that fun, isn't that great, maybe it's even pretty disappointing sex. Sometimes first-time sex in *particular* isn't that great, because, well, it's your first time and you are learning and likely your partner is learning, too. Disappointing, blah sex, "learning sex" is a part of life and just about all sexually active relationships. It's a part of marriage. Just because you are having sex with someone you are married to doesn't guarantee that it will be good sex. Being in a relationship with someone you love can certainly help the sex be good sex a lot of the time, but loving someone simply doesn't guarantee good sex in general. (And, marriage and a committed relationship aren't guaranteed protections against sexual violence either—more on this later.)

Having *respect* for sex (in general) and *respect* for your partners (in general) *will* go a long way toward the end of fostering good, fulfilling sex and a respectful relationship with your partners overall, one which promotes a sense of mutual value and care about consent. And whether or not you are a virgin is irrelevant on this front. Virgins and nonvirgins alike should aim to develop a healthy respect for all sex and all partners. Whether they are the first, the second, the fiftieth, or the only partners you have in your lives.

Gossip About Sex Is Toxic

Since we are on the topic of labels and categories, I want to take a moment to circle back to the name-calling issue, like I did in the chapter about girls and women. Name-calling around sex usually makes girls and women its victims, and takes the form of slut-shaming.

The slut-shaming of anyone—no matter how much they've had sex and with how many partners—is always and everywhere unacceptable. Gossiping about who is having sex with whom, or who is having a lot of sex, or not enough sex, is always and everywhere unacceptable. Calling people prudes for not having enough sex or not having any sex is always and everywhere unacceptable.

Gossip, slut-shaming, name-calling—all of it is toxic.

Gossip, slut-shaming, name-calling is poisonous.

The surest way to hurt another person, to demean them, to disrespect as a fellow human, to disregard their worth and well-being is to gossip about this very intimate, vulnerable aspect of human experience and identity—it's to slut-shame them. The surest way to reinforce the problematic hierarchies in our culture for men and women that force everyone into Oscar-worthy performances—and alienate all of us from who we really are—is to gossip, label, and slut-shame.

And slut-shaming is often racist.

Black, Latina, and other minority women and girls are more likely to be victims of gossip and slut-shaming than white women because non-white women and girls are often stereotyped as more promiscuous. Rich, white women are the least likely to be slut-shamed, so economic status can influence whether you are more or less likely to be slut-shamed. Educational background can influence slut-shaming. Basically, the more privileged you are, the less likely you are to be slut-shamed. Though it's also true that *all* women and girls—whether white, wealthy, and super-privileged or not, just for the mere fact of being women and girls—are vulnerable to slut-shaming. Slut-shaming and name-calling generally start with gender bias and goes from there. Sigh. Depressing I know.

So don't be a part of it!

You Are Cordially Invited: The New Big (Sex) Questions

At the beginning of this book, I suggested a long list of Big Questions, including this one:

What does it mean to be a sexual being?

I want to come back to this question now.

Whenever I am giving a talk about sex and consent to students, I extend the invitation to devote some time, effort, and thought about who they are as sexual beings. I ask the kinds of questions we've been exploring here, like, What is good sex? I encourage everyone in the audience to spend at least one semester of their college experience taking advantage of the resources—both human and educational—that they have available to them on their campuses, toward the end of better understanding who they are as sexual beings, what they might want from sex, and who they hope to be as partners.

Absolutely anyone can participate in this kind of reflection—no prior sexual experience is required. This kind of contemplation is inclusive of all kinds of ideas about sex and it doesn't discriminate based on whether or not you are a virgin. It doesn't even presume you've ever kissed anybody before! All it requires is that you be a human being, and one who is open and interested in the aspect of your humanity that is your sexuality.

So I want to formally extend this invitation to you now.

You are cordially invited to wonder:

What does it mean to be a sexual being?
What is good sex?

Welcome, welcome to all who are reading! These questions are for you, and you, and you and you and *you*. No RSVPs necessary.

Some Contemplative Calisthenics:

1. To contemplate these two very important and complex questions, I want you to read, I want you to watch television and movies, take walks and ponder, talk to your friends, talk to the adult mentors in your life that you've identified as trustworthy. (And lucky for you, there is a list of suggested readings in the back of this book!) *And*, if you are comfortable enough, I want you to talk to your parents. I want you to ask how they might answer these two questions themselves, and what things they've read, watched, or thought about that might help you better understand your own answers, or expand your thinking about them.

2. Now I want you to spend some time thinking about where you've gotten your ideas about sex before reading this book. It's important for us to identify where from and what we've been taught about sex. What are your sources? (Name as many as you can think of. For example, maybe it's a movie you saw, maybe it's what you were taught by your religious tradition, maybe you took sex ed in school, maybe your friends told you something, maybe you've watched porn, maybe your parents had a talk with you, maybe your siblings did.)

Now I want you to spend some time *judging* those sources. Go through them one by one. Do you agree with what you learned? Do you disagree? Why/why not?

It's important to remember that lots of people will give you their opinions about how you should be and act with respect to sex. One of the most important tasks for *you* in this book, though, is for *you* to decide where you are in relation to those opinions and teachings. You have the right to judge and differ from these opinions—in fact, it's really important that you take the time to do this. It's *your right* and your obligation to yourself. It's part of how choices about sex open up before you, and sex becomes something important to you, rather than the opposite.

3. On the subject of gossip, labels and slut-shaming. Remember how I keep saying that I want you to become critical thinkers about yourselves? Remember that relational ethic you have with regard to your friendships and familial relationships? Let's call up that relational ethic again and with it, all that critical thinking and self-reflection about who you are and who you really want to be.

Ask yourself now: Does gossip, slut-shaming, and name-calling hold up to your relational ethic? Does it hold up to the respect that you believe you should show to a good friend? To how you want to communicate their value to them? Does it hold up to how you hope to be treated by others, too?

If the answer is no to any of these questions, then you already know what you are called to do here. Enough said.

Why Are People So AFRAID of Sex? Why Is There So Much Shame Around Sex?

DANGER! Don't Go in There! (Danger, Danger, DANGER!)

So, are *you* afraid of sex?

Have you been raised to not really talk about it? Do the people around you at school get all hush-hush about it or make it into something you're not supposed to talk about? Are your parents terrified that you might have sex?

We've already talked a bit about fear, especially in relation to not *performing* masculinity and femininity according to stereotype, or the ways that religion fears gender nonconformity and sexual diversity. But here we are going to zero in on fear of sex *in general*.

And if you answered *yes* to any of the above questions, there's a reason for this:

Sex is a big deal. Sex has consequences. Sex is not something to be treated lightly. There are lots of things that can happen when you become sexually active.

Here are the biggest scary ones, which I'm sure you know already:

1. Pregnancy (if you are engaged in heterosexual intercourse).

2. STIs (sexually transmitted infections).

3. Sexual violence/assault.

You can't just shrug your shoulders at these things. They are all *big deals*.

The adult people in your life don't want you to experience a pregnancy when you are not ready, or any of the other possible negative health consequences that can arise from having sex. The adult people in your life don't ever want you to be the victim of sexual violence or the perpetrator of it either. Your parents' fears, if they have them, are justified. Your teachers, your mentors, your coaches, the other important adult figures in your life—their worries are justified, too.

But . . . But . . . ! (There's always a *but!*)

Those fears are justified *to a point.*

The big problem is that, because their fears about *you* having sex can become huge and sprawling like some horrible, enormous, lurking monster, the potential, negative, dangerous consequences of sex also can eclipse all other things about sex like the moon in front of the sun. To the point where the good of sex, its positive consequences, we kind of forget to tell you about that part. And so much of what is offered to you as sex ed is, well, basically, "Warning, warning, WARNING!!!!! Bad things might happen if you have SEX! Like, super, *super* bad!"

And while this *is* true, it's absolutely not the only possible consequence of you having sex. I don't want fears about sex to become like a fortress blocking out all the positive, especially because fear can get in the way of you becoming the sexually empowered, self-aware, and self-possessed person I want you to become. So many possible consequences of becoming sexually active *are* positive. Just a few of the possible *positive* consequences of you having sex include: love, relationship, pleasure, happiness, connection, and like, a whole lotta fun.

Girls, Sex, and Fear

We need to talk about girls and women again.

It's impossible for us to talk about the dangers and warnings people offer us about sex and not also talk about girls and women (in general) and girls' and women's bodies (in particular) because:

* Girls' and women's bodies bear the consequences of unplanned pregnancies.

* Girls and women are most likely to be the victims of sexual violence.

* Girls' and women's bodies are most likely to be the sites of sexual violence.

There is no getting around these realities. Girls and women bear the brunt of the negative and potentially dangerous consequences that make people afraid of sex—disproportionately so. It's a burden that girls and women bear their entire lives. It is a truth of our world. It makes being a girl-bodied and girl-identitied sexual being more complicated. Sigh.

This is why so much of the fear and danger-based sex ed is directed *especially* toward girls and women. Parents don't want their daughters to end up dealing with an unplanned pregnancy. (Of course they don't!) Parents don't want their daughters to be the victims of sexual violence. (Of course they don't!)

But one of the consequences of *this* is that girls and women end up being raised to believe that it is their sole job to:

A. Prevent pregnancy.

B. Prevent themselves from being sexually assaulted.

Boys and men are not always educated about the potential consequences and dangers of sex in the same way. Boys and men don't have to worry about getting pregnant, so their attitude about sex can be completely different—more free, more liberated (in theory) because it's not their bodies that will carry a pregnancy should a pregnancy occur. The worst part is, we often *allow* them to believe they don't have to worry about pregnancy since it's not their bodies that will carry the pregnancy. It becomes the woman's job to be on the Pill, the woman's job to make sure some sort of birth control is used during sex, and the woman's job to say *no*: No, we shouldn't; no, we can't do that; no, that's not a good idea. *Yes,* you need to wear a condom!

It becomes the woman's job to *stop* a pregnancy.

Until recently, education around sexual violence has been offered primarily to women and girls, despite the fact that statistics show that men are typically the perpetrators of sexual violence.

Girls and women are offered (well-meaning) advice:

* Don't walk home late at night by yourself.

* Don't go home with anyone you don't know very well.

* Don't go to this or that frat party because that frat is known as the "Rape House."

* Don't drink too much because drinking makes a woman vulnerable to assault.

When sexual violence prevention education is offered primarily to women and girls, this sends a message that it is the *woman's job* to stay away from situations that might make her vulnerable to assault. This sends a big, loud message to women: If you are the victim of sexual violence, then it *must be your own fault.* You must have done something stupid to put yourself at risk. Therefore *you brought that violence upon yourself.*

And *this* tendency has led sexual violence prevention advocates everywhere—and angry people everywhere—to ask things like:

Why is it a *woman's* responsibility to prevent her own rape? Why aren't we educating boys and men not to become rapists? What about *that?* Why can't we educate boys and men *not to sexually assault* the woman they see walking home late at night or the woman they met at a party and went home with or the woman who has passed out on the couch from drinking?

Pretty good questions, right?

This biased approach to prevention education implies that it's the woman's responsibility to prevent herself from being raped as opposed to *the guy's responsibility to not rape her.* And this makes me really, *really* mad. I hope it makes *you* mad, too, however you identify in terms of gender.

It is only *very* recently that our culture and our schools and universities have begun to shift their sexual violence prevention education to include boys and men. But more on this in the consent chapters. And to sum up here: If you're a girl or a young woman, then society is unfortunately going to be tougher on you—and more fearful *for* you. It's not fair. I know.

Religion-Based Fears

We are back to the topic of religion *again.*

(I know, I know: It's everywhere, isn't it?)

And wow. Where to begin with this one?

With very rare exceptions, and very, *very* unfortunately, much of what religions teach young adults about sex is negative and fear-based. I mean, we could be here all day discussing how. This *entire book* could be about how religions have negatively influenced sex education, views of women in relation to sex and their bodies, and societal attitudes based on gender and sexual identity.

But, before I move forward, I want to be clear: There is *plenty* within religions and their corresponding theologies and traditions that is positive about sex. Tons of good stuff there! I mean, have you ever read the Song of Songs / Song of Solomon in the Old Testament? Or done any research on Rati and Kama, the Hindu goddess and god? Pretty racy stuff! And there's so much more where that came from, in just about any religious tradition you can name.

However.

Generally, religions have *very particular contexts* where and with whom all that sexy, lusty goodness is okay to experience. You guessed it: within heterosexual marriage! There are a few exceptions to this rule, but these are recent developments on the religion front. The deal for just about forever has been that the only place for sex according to religions is heterosexual marriage. Yup. Sorry. All other circumstances? Nope. Not allowed. You risk displeasing whatever divinity or divinities your tradition believes in if you ignore this edict, and you will have done some serious mortal sinning if you happen to be Catholic (and mortal sinning is not a good thing).

I am not trying to be disrespectful to religion and I am not against religion. If I could write this entire book and talk about only positive, wonderful, empowering things that religions have offered us with respect to sex and consent, I'd love to do it. There are so many things I love about my own family's Catholic tradition, its symbols, its rituals, its spiritual practices, and its theologies (especially the feminist, liberation, mujerista, and womanist traditions).

But for our purposes here, it's imperative (read: *required*) to grasp the extent of religions' influence on our society and culture's very negative, very fearful, very unable-to-talk-and-teach-about-sex-in-positive-ways attitude. Religions, particularly the Christian traditions, have an enormous influence on how *you* have been educated about sex (or *not* educated about sex as the case may be), *even if your family is not religious at all* (I know—weird, right? How did that happen?). There is no escaping religion's influence on what you learn about sex growing up. This may not be obvious on the surface of the sex education you've been offered, but trust me, religion's influence *is* there. It's baked right in, like the chocolate chips in chocolate chip cookies.

Religions, particularly Christian traditions, have influenced this country's (and most Western countries') laws, this country's politics, history, culture, societal attitudes and values and everything else you can imagine since this country was born, especially our ideas about sex, gender, and sexual identity. This means that how we talk to and educate *or don't talk to and educate* kids about sex and gender is highly influenced by this history.

When I was doing my research about sex on campus, I asked everyone I interviewed who claimed a particular religious affiliation what their tradition taught them about sex while growing up.

The vast majority answered with sarcastic laughter. They snickered and they railed against the sex ed from their traditions. They either summed up that education as a prohibition, "Don't do it," or complained they'd had no sex education whatsoever because in their tradition, you aren't supposed to talk about sex. (The only exceptions were the liberal Jews, who told me their tradition taught them that sex is a positive thing, that pleasure is important, especially women's pleasure, and that if they had sex outside of marriage, they felt like people at their synagogue would be okay with that, including the rabbi. Go Jews!)

Most people felt like their traditions were overwhelmingly negative about sex, and worse, if they were taught anything at all (many people weren't), it was that to have sex is shameful (unless you are married). Most students also felt angry about their traditions' anti-gay stances. (This was another thing students told me they'd "learned" from their traditions, especially students who identified as Catholic or evangelical Christian: "Don't be gay.")

Not good stuff. Not good at all.

Gender bias was also a big issue. Religions are particularly focused on women in relation to sex and sin. (I mean, *Eve*, okay?) Women are considered temptresses who draw men into sexual sin. (Go ladies!) Though religions usually expect men *and* women to follow their traditions' expectations about sex outside of heterosexual marriage, men, generally, are not judged or punished for this in the same ways women are. Women tend to be judged (and gossiped about) more harshly, and the consequences for women not following their faith's laws around sex can be lifelong. (They may not be considered worthy of marriage, for example, or even of remaining alive. And I'm not even going to get into stoning women for having been raped. Yes, that still happens in our world today.)

Ugh, ugh, *ugh*.

Religions are in large part responsible for the enormous shame that so many of us—women especially—experience around sex. The ways we hide that we've had sex. The fact that it's difficult to talk about sex in our culture, sometimes even taboo to talk about it, depending on where you are and who you are with. Religions tend to be shame factories on this issue.

And shame with respect to sex is *never* a good thing.

Fear and Shame Go Hand in Hand (and Not in a Romantic Way)

We need to talk more about shame.

A big thing I've learned from my conversations with young adults over the years is that people feel buckets, absolute *buckets* of shame around sex. We tend to be *swimming* in shame. Oh, let me count the ways and whys of that shame like it's a sonnet! (Kidding. I couldn't write a sonnet. I'm not that talented.)

* People feel ashamed for being a virgin.

* People feel ashamed for *not* being a virgin.

* People feel ashamed when talking about sex.

* People feel ashamed for not knowing how to talk to their sexual partners about sexual things.

* People feel ashamed for not having *enough* sex.

* People feel ashamed for having *too much* sex.

* People feel ashamed for feeling undesirable and unwanted.

* People feel ashamed for desiring their partners to like-them, like-them.

* People feel ashamed for wanting sex and love to go together.

* People feel ashamed for wanting to be loved.

* People feel ashamed for wanting to emotionally connect to their partners.

* People feel ashamed for having been a victim of sexual violence.

- ✳ People feel ashamed for wanting to only kiss.

- ✳ People feel ashamed for liking sex too much.

- ✳ People feel too ashamed to ask their sexual partner to give them an orgasm.

- ✳ People feel ashamed of teaching their sexual partners to give them an orgasm.

- ✳ People feel ashamed of never having had an orgasm.

- ✳ People feel ashamed of masturbating.

- ✳ People feel ashamed of *admitting* they masturbate.

I mean, JEEZ. This list could go on as long as Long Island! The thing about shame is that it doesn't just turn our faces red. Shame is toxic. Yes, it's another one of those toxic things, like gossip. Shame ends up hurting us and sometimes it hurts other people, too.

These kinds of shame tend to grow out of our fears, and often we are *taught* those fears. We inherit them from societal, cultural, and religious biases.

Here comes my fear-shame poem:

- ✳ We're afraid if we admit we want to be loved by our partners, they'll reject us and leave us.

- ✳ We're afraid if we ask our partners to give us an orgasm, they'll laugh in our faces or simply refuse.

*   We're afraid that we don't really know how to have sex and we're afraid to look up some advice because if we do this, we're admitting we don't really know what we're doing.

*   We're afraid if we masturbate our parents might catch us.

*   We're afraid of being humiliated somehow.

*   We're afraid our bodies are ugly and undesirable.

*   We're afraid other people will judge us for having sex, for not having sex, for having too much sex, for being bad at sex.

*   We're afraid of our parents finding out we've had sex.

*   We're afraid that if our religious communities find out we've had sex, they'll call us sinful and unworthy in an unredeemable, unfixable way.

*   We're afraid of the consequences of having sex, like getting pregnant, and then having to deal with those consequences.

I could keep going and going but I'll stop there.
But you get the idea.
We've got a lot of baggage, don't we?
The problem with all this shame and fear is silence. Shame and fear silence us. And silence with respect to sex is also *never* a good thing.

Silence leads us to tamp down our feelings and to pretend they aren't there. Silence leads to isolation with big stuff we shouldn't be alone with. Silence also leads to not-so-good sex, doing things we don't really want to do (yikes! consent!), an absence of pleasure and orgasms, an absence of connection with our partners, and often, whether we mean this or not, a lack of respect for our partners and theirs for us. Silence can lead to sexual violence. And during all that silence, we often do a lot of performing of people we are not. Silence, shame can foster a lot of pretending (more on performing and pretending later).

I do *not*—I repeat, do *not*—want you to be silent on the subject of sex.

So we really need to tackle that shame.

The Examined Sex Life Is the Healthiest Kind of Sex Life

The whole point of this book?

It's pretty much an effort to help you *articulate* stuff around sex and consent. To help you *not* be silent. To help you become self-aware (which requires acknowledging and articulating stuff to yourself) about sex and consent and to find conversation partners in your life for this subject. To do all of this, to *not* be silent, requires us to face our fears and our shames. It probably requires our parents and conversation partners to do this, too.

Fears and shames around sex are common, even among the adults in your life. Probably *especially* among a lot of the adults in your life. We all have fears and shames. I have them. No one escapes them! Some of them are simply part of being human. They come from us having bodies that change and feelings that we don't know what to do with or how to control, and the fact that heartbreak is a part of life. But some of these come from those problematic biases in culture, society, and religion which end up being toxic to us. So while some fear and shame is normal, a lot of fears and shames are *not* and they can be destructive.

The key to contending with the destructive kinds of fears and shames involves finding a healthy balance in your life with respect to this stuff. There's a healthy amount of fear and worry we experience around sex because we are only human. But we don't want to tip into that unhealthy place, where fears and worries become shames that are toxic to us and ultimately to our partners.

How do we find that balance?

You guessed it:

By becoming critical thinkers.

By asking Big Questions and then asking them again.

By allowing the task of figuring out sex and our sexualities to be an *ongoing journey*—one where we get accustomed to coming back to it, again and again, in the effort to reflect, to wonder, to ponder about what is happening and what we are feeling and why. We do this by becoming humans who *seek understanding* about sex, who understand that the *examined sex life* is the approach to sex that will help us to remain as healthy as we can attempt to be in this complicated but beautiful area of our humanity.

So *yes*, I am calling on our friend Socrates once again!

Because I believe that knowing, investing in, and taking the time and effort required to think and think again about all-things-sex and all-questions-sex can shift the balance from an unhealthy amount of fear, shame, and silence toward a *healthy,* positive, and life-affirming place where you can be and become on this issue.

Rather than *fearful*, I'd prefer that you be *respectful* of this part of who you are—of this aspect of your being and also its potential, very life-changing consequences. To have a *healthy respect* for sex and all that it implies for you and for your partners is a positive way to acknowledge the fact that sex *is* a big deal, and there is no getting around this fact. Rather than *ashamed*, I'd prefer that you become *confident* in yourself around issues related to sex. I'm not talking about confidence as in arrogance. I am not advocating that you become this boastful, know-it-all. (Gosh, no! Don't do that!) But when we have a *healthy confidence* we are not alone and silent. We can articulate what we need, emotionally and physically, and we can ask honest questions when we aren't sure what we need, emotionally and physically. We become thoughtful people who know that to be a sexual being is to be a thinking being, a flexible being, a being who listens and asks questions and understands that sex is a complicated aspect of our humanity.

Because *there is no shame* in being who you are, and part of who you are is a sexual being.

There Is No One-Size-Fits-All Sexuality (Really)

I know I've already said this a bunch of times, but because we're talking about fear and shame, I feel like it's important to say this again and say it right here.

The biggest mistake I see everywhere—the biggest mistake I think our culture and society and religions have made over the century with respect to sex—is this: trying to offer, or really, *to enforce*, a single vision of what it means to be a sexual being. As in, one framework, one unique method or path for being sexual, for expressing sexuality, even for how and why to have sex.

The One-Size-Fits-All model for sexuality.

Kind of like those one-size-fits-all T-shirts and sweatshirts you sometimes see. They are supposed to fit *everybody*, and, in reality, they fit *nobody*.

Unfortunately, most of us have grown up with this model and have been taught that we must *force ourselves* to somehow fit into this vision, even if doing so makes us miserable, if it feels entirely wrong, and even if it means we must deny who we really are to others, to ourselves, to try and become someone we are not and should never try to be.

This reality is *tragic*.

This one-size-fits-all sexuality that most of us are offered is so narrow, so tiny, so extra-extra-extra-*extra* small that it squeezes most of us until we cannot breathe. And some of us until we no longer want to live. It tends to fit only certain heterosexual people who can wait to become sexual individuals until they are in a heterosexual marriage. For those people who feel comfortable within that framework, one-size-fits-all is great!

But listen: If you are someone for whom it does *not* fit, I want you to take off that ridiculously sized sweatshirt right now, this minute. Get that uncomfortable sexuality shirt off your body, fold it, and put it back in the drawer where it belongs. Or recycle it. Let it go!

I believe that everybody is different (even if your one-size-fits-all-sexuality sweatshirt fits you perfectly—you just got lucky). I believe that part of the work of figuring out what it means to be a sexual being and the meaning of sex is that it is, well, *work*. We need to figure it out. It's kind of like we each need to sew our own sweatshirts so they fit uniquely to our bodies and our beings and our sexualities. It requires investment and searching and explorations and journeying and reevaluation of our route along the way (so you might need to update and expand that sweatshirt as you get older—let out the seams a bit).

The whole point of this book is to help you find a sexuality and an understanding of sex and consent that is roomy and flexible enough to accommodate the unique person that you are and the complexity of relationships and partners you will have during your lifetime. I want it to be a sexuality that empowers you, that frees you, that makes you feel joyful and hopeful and that can comfort you when you are not feeling that way. So if the one you're wearing now makes you feel awful and ugly and terrible, then *take it off.* I mean it! Right now. Do it. Don't be afraid. Don't be ashamed. I'll turn my back.

For Some Shameless Searching:

Write down a list of any fears you have around sex, or fears that people have expressed about sex in relation to you. (Consider your parents, your teachers, family members, religious leaders, etc.). Now think about if/how your gender identity influences these fears. Next think about if/how your family's religious affiliation (if you have one) has influenced these fears.

Now I want you to think about shame. Do you have any "shames" associated with sex, love, relationship? If so, write each one down. Is there anything you are afraid of talking to someone about with respect to sex? Please write down each thing, and write a little about why you are afraid to say it out loud.

Next I want you to think about ways, opportunities, resources that might help you overcome these fears, these shames, these silences. Consider all the ways that you and the people around you hide about sex. Where are the safe spaces in your life—the people, the literal places, the books and shows you read and watch—where you might work through some of this stuff? Try to think of as many as you can and write down that all-important list.

What Is Your Sexual Ethic? What Does It Have to Do with Consent?

Reckoning with That (Sexual) Ethics Allergy

Do your eyes water when you hear the term "sexual ethics"?

Or maybe you get hives all over your body. Or you sneeze. Or you turn and run in the other direction. Or you just scrunch up your face in disgust. Maybe your parents do this, too. Maybe everyone around you does. Maybe you think that sexual ethics is the kind of thing that people worried about back in the fifties, before the sexual revolution. Maybe you think anything that links sex and ethics is, by definition, going to be repressive, restrictive, and downright prohibitive. The very embodiment of disempowerment. Something you need to get away from and quick, if you want to have a sex-positive future.

Remember when you were starting out on your relational ethic, I mentioned how lots of people in our culture seem kind of allergic to the word *ethics*?

Yeah. Ethics. Ethics, ethics, ethics! Mwah-ha-ha!

Well, this sexual ethics allergy that maybe you suffer from? That you feel gives good sex a bad name? Like I said before about ethics in general: relational, sexual ethics are *essential* for your sexual health and well-being and the sexual health and well-being of all your future partners. So take your allergy medication.

Why Everyone Needs Sexual Ethics

There *is* a good reason some of us feel allergic.

Typically, if we are taught anything about sexual ethics, these ethics are *imposed* on us. They are oversimplified and given to us as a set of dos and, even more likely, as a set of *don'ts*. What often passes as sexual ethics involves *prohibitions* around sex, LGBTQ identity, as well as abortion. Sexual ethics—which most often is done and advocated in the context of theology and religions (yup, religion again!)—is often presented as reasons for *not* having sex and reasons to stay "pure" (though not always—there is some great, feminist, theological ethics out there). It's very sex-*negative* as opposed to sex-*positive*. And we are rarely offered the chance to *participate* in developing this code of sexual ethics ourselves because people are afraid of what we might decide on our own behalf.

No wonder lots of people hear the word *ethics* with respect to relationships and sex and want to run in the other direction! No wonder people get really angry and just want to toss the whole ethics thing out into the trash!

If *you* feel that way, I totally get it—I really do.

But sexual ethics is *not* just a bunch of prohibitions around sex.

Or, it doesn't *have* to be.

And if you've just gone and recycled that one-size-fits-all-sexuality sweatshirt or put it away in a dark corner of your wardrobe, we *need* to find you a framework for sexual ethics that fits you well, that's stretchy and comfy and accommodating.

Part of how we've gotten *here*, to this place where so many of us have developed this allergy to sexual ethics? It's because political and religious liberals have pretty much given the conversation about sexual ethics away to religious and political conservatives. As though liberals have no alternative to offer!

That just isn't true. Liberals have tons to offer.

What we, what this world, what *you* are in dire need of is an alternative sexual ethical framework that is sex-positive, that prioritizes consent, and that truly empowers *you* to become a liberated, confident, healthy sexual being. We need to work toward a new sexual ethic—one that offers a clear alternative to the politically and religiously conservative one if that's not your bag.

Because I want you to have a strong sense of sexual ethics. You need one. We all do.

Lucky for you that you've already articulated a relational ethic. That's going to help you a lot as we move forward.

Building Your Own Compass: Developing Your Sexual Ethic

You know what a compass is, right?

That thing you take with you on a camping trip that always points north? That is there to help if you get lost? That's really handy if you happen to be on a sailboat?

A sexual ethic should function like a compass, pointing you in the right direction if you're feeling lost, or helping you decide what's next in a situation where there are many possible directions you might go. A Sexual Compass can be super useful.

Wouldn't it be awesome if there was this thing you could hold in your hand and consult whenever you had a dilemma about this stuff?

Like . . . Hey, Compass! Here's the situation: I really like this person, she and I have been best friends for two years, she knows me well and makes me feel understood, and we've been making out for three months now, but we haven't figured out if we're in a relationship. She isn't sure if she's ready for sex and I'm not sure either. Why aren't we ready, Compass? What circumstances need to be in place before we are?

Ideally, your Compass would sort of spin around, pointing you in different directions—maybe toward a trusted friend or two with whom you could talk this through, some resources for reflection, some questions you might ask your partner, and toward taking more time until you both feel ready.

This kind of compass would be fantastic!

(I would totally line up to buy one of those at Target the day after Thanksgiving.)

This kind of compass would help you ask the questions that need asking, seek out the conversations that could be clarifying, identify the most trusted people in your life with whom to have those conversations, help you figure out timing, and even decide the circumstances that would work well for the occasion (like sex after a nice dinner? Or just whenever the mood strikes?). This kind of compass would help you identify all the voices of others in your head that are pressuring you one way or the other around sex, pushing you toward behaviors and choices that may not feel right. This kind of compass would help to cut through all that noise so you could hear the voices of *your* heart, *your* mind, *your* soul, and *your* body—and the voices of your partners, too.

I'm happy to say that you've already got a lot of the tools you need for putting together this trusty Sexual Compass. Your relational ethic is the stuff upon which you can build your own sexual ethic, one that is sex-positive, inclusive of all types of identities for yourself and others, and big enough and stretchy enough to fit the *you* that you are, just right. In more good news, consent is going to end up being a natural built-in there, kind of like the bookshelves you might have in your living room or bedroom. Huzzah!

So, take out that relational ethic of yours right now so we can start putting together all the pieces.

Got it? Ready? Let's go!

Essential Ingredients When Building a Sexual Ethic

Below is a list of essential elements for a sexual ethic. They are not intended to be restrictive or prohibitive, but instead empowering, accommodating, flexible, sex-positive, inclusive, and consent-respectful of you and of your partners—there to help send you on your way as you construct this compass.

Flexibility. As you grow and change, as your partners change, you need an ethic that can grow and shift and accommodate. Flexibility can also open us to the differences our partners may bring to a relationship.

Respect for Sex and for One's Partner. Respect for sex, sexuality, and sexual activity and respect for your partner, for the body of your partner, and for your own body. Pretty basic stuff.

Belief in the Dignity of All Persons. All persons, no matter who they are, no matter what their background, are to be treated with dignity. When dignity and respect exist, consent will follow.

Attention to Self and Care for Physical and Emotional

Well-Being. It's important to listen to yourself, to your gut, to that internal voice of yours telling you what feels right and what does not. You must listen to your body, to what your body tells you, to what you heart tells you, too. Bodies, hearts, minds—they all have a place in a person's sexual ethic.

Attention and Care for Physical and Emotional Well-Being of One's Partner. No matter what else anyone tells you, or how "casual" our culture expects you to be about sex and your partner, your partner is *never* an object. Do not objectify your partner; do not treat them like they do not matter. Your partner, their bodies, their desires, their needs always matter and are necessary to respect for sex to be consensual.

Open and Honest Communication and Willingness to Listen. For sex to be good, for sex to be pleasurable, for sex to be consensual, open and honest communication is essential. You need to be listened to, and your partner does, too. Make space for this kind of communication within sexual and relational intimacy.

A Commitment to Nonviolence. I hope this one doesn't need explaining!

Respect for the Complexity of This Aspect of Our Humanity. I am guessing you know this by now.

Empathy and Compassion for Self and Other. Have empathy for the needs and wishes and situations and backgrounds of your partners. Have compassion for their worries, their hang-ups, their issues. Sex can make us insecure and uncertain, and we need to practice empathy and compassion toward others, and ask for this in return.

Inclusive and Respectful of Sexual Diversity. Regardless of your sexual orientation, I want you to respect the sexual diversity of humanity and of the people who populate your life now and in the future. Sexual diversity also includes a diversity of attitudes about sex, a diversity of paths, a diversity of timelines. Sexual diversity includes more than sexual identity—*you* are part of what makes human sexuality diverse because there is *no one-size-fits-all* sexuality for any of us.

Inclusive and Respectful of Religious Diversity. You may or may not be religious, but you will meet people whose traditions will ask of them practices and timelines that may be different than your own. You need to respect those differences—unless they conflict with someone's basic human rights (such as identifying as LGBTQ and being fully practicing sexual beings as LGBTQ persons).

Since you already have your relational ethic written out, I want you to redo those lists, this time asking yourself the following questions about *partners*: those people with whom you have already or that you may in the future become sexually intimate. By intimate, I am including holding hands, kissing, spending time with, and yes, eventually, potentially having sex with.

* What does it mean to be a good partner?

* What does it mean to feel like a good partner?

* What might it look like to *not* be such a good partner?

* What might it feel like to be or to have a not-so-good partner?

* How do I want to treat my partners and how would I like them to treat me?

* What might the circumstances be that foster good, respectful sexual intimacy?

These questions may not be easy to answer or seem quite as obvious to you as the ones you asked about friendship. But they are important for you to keep in mind as you begin to develop the sexual ethic that fits you on this journey—and one where prioritizing consent is already baked right in.

A Note on You and Your Conversation Partners

Some of us are surrounded by resources for our sex education: openhearted parents, loved ones, mentors, great friends, teachers, and family members, and lots of books and opportunities for diving into our thinking on this complicated issue. Some of us don't have this, not because there aren't loved ones in our lives or people who care, but because this topic can be tough to talk about throughout our lives, not just when we are young. But it's also possible that this topic is taboo in your family or even in your community, and you feel alienated and alone, rejected and angry.

If you look around and see that the resources for thinking about sex and consent and for developing your sexual ethic are scarce, I want you to know that you are not alone.

For one, you have *you*. Okay. So, I know that sounds like a silly thing to say, but I mean it. *You* are your very own resource— you are. You *know* things—you know things about relationships. You know more than you think you know. You *know* how to have a good friendship and when you are being a not-so-good friend. You can identify the good in people and the good in yourself. You have an internal voice (a compass baked right in!) that is rejoicing on your own behalf when you've done the right thing and that is nagging at you when your decisions aren't the best ones. This voice is also there to tell you when you are feeling isolated and rejected that *you are good, you are worthwhile*, that whomever you feel attraction to and however you identify, *this is okay* and *this is good, too*.

The key is to learn to listen to that voice, to *trust* it.

To see the *authority* in it. To recognize that we each have our own authority within us—and the power that goes with it. I want you to learn to become self-aware about your *own power* because *you do have power*.

So much of what we need to be healthy people around the issues of sex and consent we already have within us. We possess it! We need to learn to see this, acknowledge it, take the time to develop our interior selves and give those selves the time and space to listen, to think, to wonder, and to articulate what we really believe.

So, *really*, I mean it: You have *you*.

And I believe in you.

It's also important that every one of us finds our way toward conversation partners about these topics. This is one of the first things I asked you to think about in this book—first because of how essential it is for you to have people you trust that you can talk to. It may take time to identify those people, but I want you to persist. I want you to make it a goal to find at least one adult and one friend you can talk to and trust, but ideally more. As many as you can identify.

Some Ethical Quandaries for You to Consider:

I want you to think about all the sexual ethics you've inherited so far from others. Try and think of anything and everything. (It might include, "Don't have sex until marriage," for example. Or it might be something like, "Sex is meant for a loving relationship.") Write down everything you can think of and from every source you can imagine—your parents, communities, schools, friends, social media, pornography. Anything at all that seems like it has to do with sexual ethics, even if you're not completely sure.

Now go through this list and place a check next to the things that make you feel really uncomfortable—that don't feel like *you* or that just don't feel right. Why do you think this is? What doesn't "fit" about them?

Next go through the "Essential Ingredients" list that I gave you for your sexual ethic in this chapter. Is there anything on that list that you feel like doesn't belong there, or conflicts with your instincts about sexual ethics? Anything that conflicts with the relational ethic you've already been working on? Or that makes you feel uncomfortable? If so, write about it in your journal, and do some reflecting about why you don't think it belongs. Try to understand what doesn't feel right about it to you.

If there aren't any elements on that list that you are resisting, I want you to take this list and put it in *order of importance* to you—rearrange the elements in your journal, in order of 1, 2, 3, etc., from most important to least important. I want you to do this because I want you to spend time thinking about and trying to understand what, with respect to sexual ethics, is your *most important priority* and why. What do *you* value most about sexual ethics?

Now I want you to think about whether I've missed anything on this list—and what that is. Something you need to add. Make sure to write down whatever it is. Then add anything you want to keep from the sexual ethics you've inherited.

ADVICE TO OUR YOUNGER SELVES PART II

"I wish someone had explained that consent has a place in various situations. I was aware that there were boundaries with my body, and that there were inappropriate ways to be touched, especially by adults. But I didn't realize those boundaries could extend to non-sexual instances, such as not wanting to hug and kiss all extended family members or people in our church community. I grew up in a big Southern family, and there was a lot of emphasis placed on showing respect and love through affection. There are other ways to show respect and love, and forcing kids to perform affection could cause them to grow up thinking they have to appease people through other forms of physical contact."

–BRANDY COLBERT, author of *The Only Black Girls in Town* and *The Revolution of Birdie Randolph*

"Dear twelve-year-old me: (1) No one ever gets to pressure you into doing something sexual you don't want to do. (2) Sex, in itself, is morally neutral. Despite what you've been told, as long as respect, mutual consideration, and mutual consent among adults is present, sex is not immoral or wrong. (3) You are allowed—even encouraged!—to pursue pleasure."

–KRISTIN CASHORE, author of *Jane, Unlimited* and the Graceling Realm series

"I'd tell my 12-year-old self to always verbalize to both myself and my partner what I wanted to happen, why I wanted that thing to happen, and then be honest with all the possible ramifications of that thing actually happening. For instance, I fell in love at 15 and our relationship was beautiful and life changing. But we never verbalized what was happening to us sexually. We just followed what our bodies wanted to do. The result was a pregnancy scare and relationship stress that we never fully recovered from. Verbalizing your desires and the risks of those desires may be awkward at first but it inspires an evolutionary leap in consciousness that will be invaluable to both personal and professional relationships the rest of your life."

–B. T. GOTTFRED, author of *The Handsome Girl & Her Beautiful Boy* and *Forever For a Year*

"I wish someone would have told me there's so many different ways to have sex and that whatever genitals you have don't have to define the kind of sex you have. If I could talk to my 12-year-old self I'd tell him that he gets to decide his own boundaries and that those boundaries deserve respect."

–ROBIN GOW

"Dear 12-year-old Keah: I think of you often. There was a lot we went through the year we turned twelve. Here I am at 28, writing to you wishing you knew then what I know now. Let me start by saying, I love you. I love you even though you've begun hating yourself. Your anger won't keep you warm in the way you're hoping. I'm sorry. I should also tell you that you're so cute it makes me teary when I see pictures of you now. You're funny, loyal, smart, and talented. Start creating now, it's good stuff. You'll believe me later because you'll love YOU later. I want the world for you. I want you to stop hardening your heart in an effort to protect it. Your vulnerability will serve you so much later. I know you want to be "normal" but there's no such thing. You're perfect just the way you are. Don't roll your eyes at me, I know it's cheesy but it's true! My #DisabledAndCute (That'll make sense later!) bean. I love you. Let others do the same. Get ready for world domination :) Love you for always, Keah."

–KEAH BROWN, author of *The Pretty One: On Life, Pop Culture, Disability, and Other Reasons to Fall in Love with Me*

"To the sheltered, Catholic school student 12-year-old me: No, not all girls 'just like the way another girl's face looks' and your friends won't all feel the same fluttering nervousness around your pretty female teachers. That's called *attraction*—and it's okay. You'll want to tell your friends you have a crush on Anthony for the next three years, but you don't, and you can stop pretending. The photos on your bedroom walls of Brad Pitt all have Jennifer Aniston in them, and one day you'll be able to just say, 'Jennifer Aniston is gorgeous, I'm attracted to her' and you'll understand those feelings. You can be, and are, attracted to girls. You always have been, and there's nothing wrong with that."

–NICOLE MELLEBY, author of *In the Role of Brie Hutchens . . .* and *Hurricane Season*

PART TWO

Other Things to Consider in Our Effort to Build That Sexually Liberated Utopia

(And That Are Really Important to CONSENT)

What Is VULNERABILITY?
Why Does It Matter?

Developing a Thinner Skin

Did you read that right? Didn't I mean *thicker* skin?

Or am I actually advocating a *thin* skin instead of a thick one?

Yes. Yes, it's very possible.

When we are small, when our parents and the people who care about us see us hurting because another person at school has said or done something mean to us, and we cry or we don't want to go back to school because of it, we might be told we need a "thicker skin" or even just a "thick skin."

The thicker our skins, the idea goes, the easier it will be for us to tune out the meanness of other people, to get over the not-so-nice things people might say to us, the times we don't get invited to the sleepover or the baseball game where the people we thought were our friends are going. A thick skin is a kind of invisible, protective shell around our hearts and the soft spots in us that are vulnerable to pain and hurt and loneliness. A thick skin can help us survive the hurts of life and make it through them to the other side.

A *thick* skin, in other words, is a *good* thing.

Up to a point.

Ideally, our skins don't become *so* thick that we are impermeable, so much that not only the bad rolls off us but the good stuff, too. If our skins get *too* thick, we become resistant to love and happiness and connection and intimacy. Our skins become like walls that let nothing else in. Or they end up numbing us to the pain and needs of others, including that of our friends and partners. That is when a thick skin becomes something that no longer serves us, that isolates us from the world and everyone else in it.

Remember how in the chapter on boys and guys I talked about how boys grow up learning that to be a "real man" means to be invulnerable? To be a jerk? To be unfeeling? That is what I am talking about here, too. Boys especially are told to make their skins as hard and impermeable as possible, but *all of us* are being raised to develop thick skins these days, which is why I want us to take another bigger-picture look at vulnerability.

Even though hurt and pain are unpleasant, they are a big part of what makes us human and what gives us the capacity to love and be loved. Our vulnerability is necessary to live a good and happy and connected life. At the root of our relationships is the willingness and capacity to be vulnerable to another person. Our willingness to, quite literally, *feel* for others. To be empathetic, sympathetic, caring. With respect to sex and consent, these qualities are essential.

Sex, consent, and relationships in general are *all* about our willingness and ability to *feel* for others—and feel for ourselves. Allowing ourselves to *feel* for others helps alert us to when those we care about need something from us, when they are hurting and in pain, and need us to offer them attention and care. It helps us become *attuned* to the pain, the hurt, the vulnerability, the needs of others, including our partners.

Consent requires this of us.

Consent is a kind of *attunement* to our partners.

We need to be attuned to them, and we want them to be attuned to us.

So, while we may be tempted to try and become invulnerable in the face of the potential hurt that seems to be everywhere around us, especially in the palms of our own hands on our smartphones (more on this later), invulnerability is not a quality that will lead us down a path to loving, fulfilling, ethical, and consensual relationships.

Vulnerability Is a Strength (We Are Not Made of Steel and That Is Good!)

Have you ever heard that phrase "to steel oneself"?

As in, I'm *steeling myself* for bad news about my interview. Or,

you'd better *steel yourself* for this conversation because she's probably going to break up with you and make you weep. *Steel*, as in
the very hard, durable metal. To "steel oneself," as in to make
oneself *like steel*, hardened, impervious, unbreakable. The kind
of thing we learn to do in the face of a world that might hurt us:
If we can just *steel ourselves* then we'll be strong (not weak), so the
theory goes. Because we never want to show our weakness (our
vulnerability)! We don't want to be caught weak, so go and make
yourself steel-like!

I've heard college students associate vulnerability with
weakness a lot.

That, to let ourselves care, to feel things deeply, to let other
people's actions make us feel sad or lonely, is to admit this very
thing, *weakness*, and to be weak is something negative. Therefore
to be vulnerable must also be negative.

And yet, vulnerability—the many ways in which we are vulnerable because of our relationships because we *do* care—is one
of the core things that make us human. We have soft sides, we
have strong yet also fragile bodies, and this softness and fragil-
ity leaves us vulnerable to hurt, to pain, to sadness, to loss. But
our soft sides also open us to beauty, to connection, to hope, to
goodness, to love, and yes, to pleasure.

In fact, so many scholars and thinkers associate vulnerability with strength and invulnerability with the opposite of
strength. Researcher and professor Brené Brown sees vulnerability as key to relationships. Without the embrace of vulnerability, we will lock ourselves out of good, healthy, fulfilling
relationships and meaningful connection. To try and make

ourselves *invulnerable* is cowardly. For Brown, to be vulnerable is the truest sign of courage a human can offer the world, another person, and themselves.

I'm with Brené Brown here: unless you learn to open yourself to vulnerability, you will forever be warding yourself off from good, fulfilling connections and relationships, and ultimately from good sex. Building walls of steel keeps people out, sure, but it also isolates you from all the good they might bring with them.

And without a *respect for vulnerability*, it will be difficult for you to become a person who also has a respect for sex and all that goes with it, and certainly a true understanding of consent and all it requires of us. To acknowledge and reckon with our own vulnerability and the vulnerability of others, to respect this human quality we all possess, should be one of the cornerstones on which we build our framework for sexual ethics, and one that we consider when we ask our Big Questions about sex and consent.

Because sex and vulnerability, consent and vulnerability, go hand and hand.

Vulnerability Leads to Intimacy, Which Leads to Connection

Vulnerability and intimacy are intimately connected. (Ha!)

Intimacy is a kind of closeness you feel with someone. A relationship that has a special intensity to it, trust, commitment, a willingness to share one's secrets, one's hopes, one's dreams. You already have intimate relationships in your life.

I hope you have lots of these.

A person with whom you have intimacy is someone you'll tell the kinds of things you won't share with anyone else: who you have a crush on, the fact that you wish your coach would move you up to the varsity team but hasn't yet and this disappoints you or makes you mad. Within intimate relationships the full range of emotions we feel as humans can be expressed without worry of rejection for expressing them. Within intimate relationships we can be sad, disappointed, angry, thrilled, triumphant, and we can even acknowledge our failings, the unbecoming things we think about the world or even other people, jealousy, envy, the kinds of emotions we wish we didn't feel but because we are human, we do.

Can you think of a person or people in your life with whom you can be this way?

Our siblings might be on this list (for example).

In theory, our parents might be on this list (that would be awesome if they are).

We certainly *could* share all sides of ourselves without worry of rejection with our parents and close family members, because parents and family should love us unconditionally. These are the people who listen to us cry and wipe our tears and watch us make mistakes and celebrate our accomplishments when we are little. But as we grow older, it can become difficult to maintain this kind of intimacy with the people raising us. As we grow up, our experience of intimacy often shifts toward our friends and eventually to our romantic partners (which is totally normal).

The kind of total openness of feeling and emotion about

which I speak is *risky*. (Like, what if someone makes fun of us? Or thinks we are weird for feeling the things we do? Or we tell them our secrets and it turns out we couldn't trust them after all and they tell other people and then we are left ashamed and humiliated? Yikes!) We might be *afraid* to engage in intimacy with anyone, period. There may be people we can name with whom we'd like to have that kind of openness and trust, but we're not sure if we have the guts to actually *practice* that kind of openness and trust and cultivate that kind of intimacy.

We need vulnerability practice, people!

In middle school and high school I had a couple of really close friends, people I thought of as my best friends, but there were limits to the intimacy we shared between us—at least on my end. One thing that absolutely terrified me was the thought of ever admitting that one of these friends had done something to hurt my feelings or make me upset. I was scared that if I told them, "Listen, when you invited this person to the movies, and that person, too, but not *me*, I felt left out," they would shrug their shoulders and not care. My greatest fear was that they would get *angry* that 1) I felt hurt or disappointed, and 2) that I had the nerve to express this out loud and maybe even expect them to apologize. I was convinced that if I ever admitted to someone they'd hurt me then this someone would show me that, ultimately, our friendship didn't really matter to them and I would lose that relationship. I was too scared to risk speaking up and saying what I really felt, so I stayed silent out of fear. I'd push down all my hurt feelings and try to get over them without ever expressing them.

Have you ever felt this way?

The thing is, intimacy always involves risk-taking. It involves opening yourself to the possibility of rejection.

And rejection sucks. There's no way around it.

But in opening ourselves up this way to someone else, we might *also* receive the thing *our heart most desires*—acceptance in all our hurt, pain, and disappointment. We might receive that apology. We might learn that this relationship, this friendship, means just as much to this other person as it means to us. We might learn that this other person values us as much as we value them. We might learn how much we are worth to this other person. We might suddenly feel seen, feel known, feel understood.

WOW. Wow, wow, *wow*.

We might experience these extraordinary, wonderful, meaningful things because of our willingness to be *vulnerable* in the face of another person. For our willingness to live with thinner skins, rather than thicker ones. And the reward of that vulnerability and the thinness of our skins is a new level of intimacy, of relationship, of trust, of connection. Of respect and care for others and their respect and care for us. And that's why vulnerability and intimacy go hand in hand and why consent and sex and vulnerability do, too.

They are all the best of friends, really.

And To Help You Open Up:

Describe a time in your life when you felt particularly vulnerable—a situation in which you felt disappointment, pain, hurt. What were the circumstances? (Were you sick? Were you alone? Did you feel rejected somehow? Did you feel exposed?) Describe your feelings in as much detail as possible.

Did anything *good* come of that vulnerable moment? Did it lead to greater connection with someone, did it lead you to open up to someone because you needed them, did it help you discover anything new about yourself or a relationship in your life? If yes, describe.

If the answer is *no*, I want you to think about why. What did you do in response to that feeling of vulnerability? Did you *steel yourself* against the situation—and therefore, against everyone around you at the time? Did you run up to your room and slam the door and refuse to talk about why you were hurting?

Now I want you to think of a situation where you felt vulnerable in a *positive* way. Where you shared of yourself something exciting or something upsetting, a hurt or disappointment you experienced, and the person with whom you shared this thing affirmed you, made you feel seen, made you feel heard. How did the relationship change because of that sharing? Was it easier the next time to share something intimate with that person?

Make a list of the fears and worries you have about being vulnerable with others, about cultivating intimacy in your relationships. Are there any specific people you feel these fears with?

Now make a list of the reasons for getting over these fears, and how you might get over them.

Why Should You CARE?
(About Anything?)

A Competition *Not* to Care

Picture this:

I'm in the Midwest on a university visit for my research. I'm having pizza with a bunch of students, the kind of pizza that come with those dips like garlic sauce and ranch. The conversation is animated as the students are trying to explain hookups, which are the dominant framework for sexual activity on their campus.

"Hookups are, like, a competition *not* to care," says one young woman at the table.

"Yeah, and whoever cares the least *wins*," chimes in another.

Everyone at the table starts laughing and nodding.

I look at them. "What?"

The two young women pop up from their seats to illustrate how hookups go. They turn their backs on each other and turn their heads toward each other over their shoulders.

"Hookups are, like, *I don't care about you*," one of the women says, with this hand-flick gesture, like she's brushing a gnat off her shoulder.

"Yeah, well, *I don't care about you either*," says the other, mimicking the shoulder flick.

They laugh again, everyone else laughs, and then they sit back down at the table to finish their pizza.

What is a hookup? you might be wondering.

College students tend to describe it like this:

In brief, a hookup is, well, *brief*. Anything from five minutes to an entire night, it involves some kind of sexual activity, anything from kissing to some form of sexual intercourse. You are supposed to be able to walk away from your partner and never have to think about or speak to them again. Oh yeah: and likely there is alcohol involved.

A *culture* of hooking up is the dominant culture around sex at most college campuses in the United States (more on this later in the hookup chapter).

As the students and I continued to eat, I asked them to explain more about what their performance meant. They told me that the norm at their school was to be casual about sex, so both hookup partners would have to prove they cared neither about the sex nor about each other.

The students also told me that they would still communicate this lack of care for their partner *even if they were totally in love with that person* and were dying to be in a relationship with them. It was too risky to reveal to a person you were interested in them (remember vulnerability?). The dominant expectation was that students would shrug off sex and their partners, and to go against this widespread attitude was too scary.

You had everything to lose, they explained. You might embarrass yourself, you might get your heart broken, and you'd end up revealing to everyone around you and, of course, to the person you were hooking up with that, gulp, you *cared*.

But what was clear to all of us sitting at that table, eating our pizza?

Hookups really *were* a performance, and one completely detached from the reality of their feelings.

When I commented to my dinner companions that it seemed counterintuitive to convince someone you might be in love with that that you felt the opposite, the students responded, *Yeah, we know. It totally does not make any sense.*

But then I asked them about consent in a hookup.

If they were so busy not caring and turning their backs on their partners, how did they know if and when their partners stopped wanting to be there? If their partners no longer wanted to participate in the hookup?

This quieted the table. The students hadn't really thought about this before. Or about how, in all that *not caring* and *competing to see who could care the least*, this very basic form of care within a sexual encounter—making sure your partner wants to participate—might get lost.

Why Are Cultural Attitudes About Caring So Negative?

Let's talk about care and caring in general.

I know, I am *certain*, that you care about many things in your life—*deeply*. You care about your dog or your cat or your turtle or your bunny. You care about your siblings and parents even if you don't want to admit this outright to them. We've already established that you care about your friends, and I'm sure if you play on a sports team, you care about your teammates and you probably care about winning, too. I could go on and on about all the stuff I know you care about, and that doesn't even include the actual *stuff* that you care about. Like your prized possessions and the way you've made your bedroom reflect who you are and what you love in life. And I bet there are probably subjects in school that you care about, sports teams you care about, even books or music or TV shows or movies that you care about.

But I also know that, with few exceptions (like maybe our pets), most of us learn to *hide* how much we care, kind of like those college students with their hookup partners. We worry that if we care too much, others will see us as weak and clingy and annoying. So we learn to *not* let others know how much we care. Showing how much we care can be dangerous. Showing how much we care can jeopardize our power in relation to other people. Showing how much we care will clue people in to when we are hurting. Showing how much we care is risky.

Yeah, that's right. It makes us *vulnerable*.

So we silence our caring.

This brings us right back to that thin versus thick skin business. Some of the silencing we do of caring helps us survive as human people vulnerable to hurt and disappointment and broken hearts. If we were totally and utterly open about every single thing that we felt—kind of like going about the world without *any skin*—that might be tough to do. Skin is meant to protect our insides, to give all the soft spots a bit of shelter.

But *totally* silencing how much we care? Hiding how much we care so completely that we appear as though we care about nothing? So we *perform* invulnerability?

That's not a good way to move through life.

And my guess?

Not caring about other people, showing others you don't care, goes against your relational ethic. Caring and showing *how* you care by inviting your friends over, asking them what's wrong if they are seeming blue, are pretty basic things that fit within the relational ethic of most people.

And yet, so many of us learn to shrug our shoulders at others, and we learn to perform those shrugs especially when it comes to our romantic partners.

Somehow, we have created a world and culture where it's acceptable to talk about how much you love your dog and pizza and playing video games, but something is wrong with you if you admit that you care about the person you are having sex with in high school and college; a world and culture where we are expected to shrug off the people we might even love and who might love us back, as though we're all made of Gore-Tex, and the possible pain and hurt (and the joy and pleasure that goes along with everything) just rolls right off like we're one big rain jacket.

Which brings us to the subject of social media and our smartphones next.

And To Show How Much *You* Care:

Make a list of ten things you care about. Anything can be on this list—your prized possessions, things you love to do, people. Anything at all that you know you care about.

Now I want you to reflect on whether or not you feeling comfortable *showing* you care about these things in front of others. Go one by one through your list of ten. Are there some things on this list that are *easier* to show you care about? (Like, is it easier to act like you care about your pet but much scarier to show you care deeply about a friend or even something that happened between you and that friend?)

Take a look at your relational ethic. How do *care and caring* (or *not caring*) apply to your sense of good and bad friendship? Did you already have "showing how much you care" on any of your lists? If not, should you add it to one or more of your lists for your relational ethic?

Last thing—and this is the toughest one. I want you to think of one activity that could show someone else in your life—someone important—that you care. Maybe it's a conversation, or maybe it involves writing a note, or maybe it's a gesture. Whatever it is, it must express, clearly, care and caring. Now I want you to take that risk, be vulnerable, and *do that thing* that expresses you care. Afterward, I want you to record how it made you feel (Embarrassed? Happy? Uncomfortable? Good?) in your journal. But ideally, for the truly courageous among us, I'd love for you to talk with this person about how and why you showed them that you care.

How Should We BE on SOCIAL MEDIA and Our SMARTPHONES?

Self-Knowledge, Smartphones, and Social Media: Think Before You Post/Text

Have you ever thought about who you are on social media and how you act?

I'm not talking about how many followers you have, or how many likes you get on an average photo or post, or your personal brand if that's your thing. I'm talking about who you are and how you act in a more *fundamental* way.

Does how you post and how you act reflect your sense of self?

Does it reflect your relational ethic?

We've been talking about both relational and sexual ethics

and how you act toward others. Just as you already know how to act the good friend and how to act the not-so-good friend (in general), so you already know how to act the good friend on social media and when you text, and snap, and vice versa.

Right?

Or do the screens between all of us while we text and post and the (possible) anonymity we have online change your behavior? Do screens enable you to act in ways you normally wouldn't if you were standing in front of someone? Has your conscience, that infamous little voice in your brain that tugs at you sometimes when you are not acting the way you know you're supposed to (your compass!) ever spoken up as you were crafting a post, getting ready to send a text, or right after you've sent it? Has your inner voice ever screamed and cried in response to a text someone has sent to *you* that was mean, ill-advised, even approaching the level of bullying? Have you ever thought to yourself, *Ouch, that hurts*, after someone—a supposed friend—sent you a photo that proves you've been left out of some event or party? Or tagged you in a post intended to let you know you weren't invited somewhere?

Today we live in a world where everyone is seeing everyone else's life, all the time, because of social media and smartphones. Social media makes it easier to plan outings with friends, to keep in touch with our grandparents and our cousins; it gives us a creative outlet for our writing and photographs. Smartphones help us with getting around town (GPS and Uber)!

But one of the big downsides is how much social media can hurt us, make us feel left out, and make us feel alone and unwanted. And how much we can use it to hurt *others*, to make them feel left out and alone and unwanted. Varying levels of bullying occur on social media; people say mean things to one another. We happen upon a post that makes us feel unsuccessful or unpopular or as if we have all the wrong clothes or don't have enough likes on our own posts. Sometimes when we see the successes, the wealth, the beauty, the popularity, and the luck of others, they seem to point out what is not in our own lives by comparison. Comparing ourselves to others can make us feel terrible.

Withstanding this kind of constant, daily onslaught is tough. The shrug becomes our defense mechanism, that thicker skin so many of us strive for and that, in theory, is meant to help shield our hearts. We work so hard not to care.

And sometimes we get good at not caring. I worry that a lot of us are getting *really* good at not caring, at shrugging, at eliminating feeling, becoming immune to one another's hurts and vulnerabilities. I worry that the rise of social media and our obsession with smartphones and screens is one of the biggest threats to our ability and willingness to be vulnerable humans in the face of other vulnerable humans.

And while I am sure your parents, teachers, and the other adults in your life have given you some sort of warning about "thinking" before you post or text, I want you to *really* think. I mean, some of the Big, Deep Thinking that goes hand in hand with those Big Questions I keep talking about. With self-knowledge and self-possession and enlightenment. Just as I want you to become a critical thinker about yourself, I want you to become a critical thinker about *who you are* on social media and your smartphone. I want you to do some serious self-examination about how social media and your smartphone are influencing how you relate (and don't) to others, and how much you show you care or pretend you don't at all.

Because this has *everything* to do with your relational and sexual ethics, even if you don't realize it quite yet.

The Big Questions for Social Media and Smartphones

I know you know that I've done lots of research about sex and relationships and college students. But I've done a lot of research about college students, social media, and smartphones, too—a big national study about this. That research grew out of all the conversations I've had over the years about *sex*! Once social media became such a constant in our lives, it also began affecting students' relationships and how they felt about themselves in relation to others.

Students started to make a distinction that intrigued (and worried) me:

The REAL me versus the ONLINE me.

As in, the *me* that I project on social media *isn't* who I really am.

Maybe you are nodding your head because you know all about the differences between who you are, really, and who you appear to be, on Instagram and when you're texting.

Students mean a lot of different things when they discuss

this gap they see between who they believe themselves to really be versus what they are posting about themselves online. But the overarching theme is this: social media is *fake*. So many students talked about how fake everything and everyone is—and how fake *they* are too.

This bothered everybody greatly.

All the students spoke of how bad it made them feel, seeing their friends act one way in person and another way on their social media accounts. People didn't like feeling like they had to be fake! They felt that it put a strain on their relationships.

Person after person also spoke of how *appearing* happy is the number one, most important expectation on social media accounts attached to their real names. The appearance of success, popularity, even wealth is something everyone is working hard to affect—toward the end of impressing college admissions officers and future employers and just about everyone else. (Which is why people think social media ends up being so fake.) People spoke of having to hide any negative emotion, even just the mention of having a bad day. Students resented this but also felt trapped by it. Everybody is in the same boat, they felt: keeping up appearances, performing these happy, successful, popular lives even if inside people are hurting and lonely.

It seems that one big thing social media is teaching us is that keeping a smile on your face even when you feel down is a general expectation. Showing vulnerability, showing you care about what other people have versus what you have, or about how no one is paying attention to you are things you need to stop doing.

A large number of students also indicated that social media and their smartphones make them feel *used*—they knew they were supposed to be the *users* of these things, but they felt the reverse was true. They felt helpless in the face of their devices and these platforms; they felt trapped, addicted, like being on a smartphone and on social media had become more like work, even homework, than anything fun, social, and pleasurable. A lot of students likened keeping their profiles and accounts updated to having a job.

Other stressors that students discussed included:

* Because of social media and texting, we already know everything that's going on with one another so it's more difficult to find things to say in person. (It makes our relationships harder because it makes conversation more difficult.)

* Social media/texting is a drama factory! It makes people get into fights. It can hurt and even end friendships and romantic relationships.

* Because of smartphones, we're expected to be available all the time, even when we're sleeping!

* Being on smartphones all the time emphasizes what people don't have, who they're not with, and how

alone people feel. It alienates people from one another and makes them feel bad.

* A degree of bullying and nastiness from others is the price of being on social media.

Social media and smartphones also teach us things like:

* Paying attention to the world and the people in it isn't worth doing. Our phones and everything on them are more important than looking up.

* It's okay if our conversations and experiences are constantly interrupted.

* Our real bodies might not be as important as the bodies/avatars we project online.

* We are the *products* of social media, just like things we might buy at the store are products (you know, milk or cereal or a car).

* Social media and our smartphones encourage us to think of ourselves as brands—to *commodify* ourselves and each other.

The downside of social media and smartphones tended to outweigh the good side for the students I interviewed. I don't want the downside to outweigh the upside for *you*.

Everything has happened *so fast* with the invention of social media, and not long afterward, the smartphone. We still haven't caught up and figured out how to right this balance to ensure these things are *mostly* positive forces in our life, and not such overwhelmingly problematic and confusing ones. We need to find a way to tip the scales in the right direction.

This brings me to the new Big Questions all of us need to add to our list:

* What does it mean to have a healthy relationship with social media and our smartphones?

* Is that healthy relationship different for everybody?

* Is it possible that, for some people, there isn't such a thing as a healthy relationship with social media and their smartphones? (And if so, what does *that* mean?)

* What does a healthy relationship with social media and smartphones have to do with sex and consent anyway?

The rest of this chapter is designed to get you started on some answers.

Social Media Objectifies Us

Social media and smartphones instill certain values in us and teach us to *devalue* things, too. These not only influence us on an individual level but are influential in our relationships with others. These values—or *devalues*—influence your ability to assign value to *yourself* and also the value you assign (or don't) to *others*. They influence your ability to assign value to your friends and to your romantic partners.

Let's take branding. The fact that we are the products of social media.

Today, it's common for people to be taught at some point in their educations how important it is to think about their brand. (If these lessons haven't happened yet, they will!) I had a student say to me during an interview: "My name is my brand." This idea is shared by so many students now. I've heard students liken themselves to Kellogg's or Ford or Nike in discussing the importance of branding themselves and promoting that brand.

Branding and commodifying ourselves *objectifies* us. It turns humans—you and me—into objects to be crafted and molded (just like you might craft a post for Facebook or Instagram or Twitter). Objects can be bought and sold or *used* to buy and sell things, like products on the shelves at a store. Objects are inanimate. Objects are not human. Objects don't have feelings.

The idea that we *should* be branding ourselves, that our names, our lives, our bodies are *products* to be promoted, teaches us to treat others as though they are not living, breathing, feeling human beings. People are no longer physical bodies standing in front of us whom we have to look in the eye and whose reactions we see in real time. It distances us from each other and makes us think of people as online profiles, in terms of numbers of likes, as though they aren't *real* people.

But I am not a profile. You aren't either.

No one is. All of us are real and all of us are human.

None of us are products or brands, no matter how much social media and our smartphones try to convince us otherwise.

Social Media–Facebook, Instagram, Twitter–Has No Heart

Somewhere, deep down, I know you know this.

But have you ever *really thought* about what it means?

Posts and photos go by us based on *algorithms,* which have no care or worry about how people will feel when they see these posts and photos. If it might be the wrong time for someone to see something, because they are feeling lonely, left out, unattractive, or because they've just suffered a terrible loss.

Algorithms are nothing more than computer formulas, lines of code.

Algorithms don't know when we are hurting—nor do they care. Algorithms don't know when we've had a bad day—nor do they care. Algorithms don't tiptoe around us like a friend or your mom might because a friend or your mom knows that you are having a hard time and wants to take care of you. Algorithms aren't kind, aren't loving, aren't worried about our well-being like another person might be. That's because algorithms aren't human, like we are.

Think about it: We are encouraged to post all our successes. But we don't control *when* our friends and the people we care about see those successes.

Imagine a situation where you got into the college of your dreams and you are thrilled and decide to post that success online. (It makes you look good, right? And you should be proud of yourself, you really should!) But your best friend in the world has gotten rejected *everywhere,* and you know they are feeling really low about this.

I am certain you would *never* take your acceptance letter, print it out, and go wave it in your best friend's face. That would be pretty heartless. You *know* it would make them feel awful, and would emphasize the fact that you have something that they don't. You would want to be more sensitive, right?

But Instagram doesn't know—and doesn't care either—that your best friend is hurting. Instagram and Twitter and every other social media account will put that acceptance letter in front of your friend's face and hold it there, even if your friend is sobbing as they look at their phone and read through all the heady congratulations people post in response to your news.

I don't want you to feel like you aren't allowed to share your successes and achievements, or to make you feel terrible. What I *want* is for you to *realize*—to become a thinker about—what you post, and what social media culture (driven by likes, shares, retweets, etc.) can encourage us to post without considering the feelings of real life persons who may be seeing those posts, and at the worst possible time. Because of the physical distance that screens provide between us, we can't see the embodied person who hurts and cries when they are scrolling online. This desensitizes us to the fact that the people on the other side of those screens have feelings. The screens between us change how we understand and value others—or how we *devalue* them. In other words, social media helps us to act as though *we* have no hearts—even if that isn't our intention.

But we *do* have hearts—we do.

You and me. All of us.

Unlike Facebook, Instagram, Twitter, we are human.

Social media and smartphones help us forget or avoid our humanity sometimes, even a lot of times, and lose sight of what our humanity requires of us. I think we need to become better people—thinking individuals, thinking *humans*—when we post, how we post, and whether we post. I want you to be *more* human, not less.

The Ethics of Sexting

"Show me your boobs!"

"Send me a dick pic!"

Yeah, I *know*. Pretty rude of me to just come out and demand something so intimate, right? Especially when we don't even really know each other!

But who cares?! I can't see you react!

(Wait—you're still a little offended? Shocked?)

Alas. This kind of thing happens all the time over text. Maybe it's already happened to you. Maybe you've done the requesting, maybe you've received the request, and maybe you've fulfilled the request, too.

And I know, I *know* how absolutely easy it is to send a boob pic request over text. You can't see that person's face, you can't even see their body. (That's the point, right? You can't see it and you want to see it!). And you just *might* be standing in the middle of a bunch of people cheering you on to ask for this photo.

"Boob pic! Boob pic! BOOB!!!! PIC!!!!!"

But what if the cheering from people involved you *actually walking up to the person*, like, in the hallway at school or in their yard, and asking this person to *show you* their boobs to your face? Like, "Hi, it's great to see you, nice dog you got there, he's really friendly, will you SHOW ME YOUR BOOBS?"

Yeah. There's little chance you'd ever have the nerve to do something like that. I'm guessing you also know that it would be a pretty ridiculous, over-the-top, vulgar, and disrespectful thing to do to somebody.

But because our smartphones make it as easy as typing in a few words and hitting *send*—you think, *Sure! Why not? I'll do it!!* The person on the receiving end of the text can always just ignore the message.

But it's just *too easy* to tap something out on a screen and send it off without thinking! Super easy! Not brave at all. The epitome of cowardice. Because we can't see the people who are affected by what we've sent. Our phones shield us from seeing exactly how uncomfortable we've made them, or unhappy, or weepy, or ashamed, or lonely. Or how pressured we've made them feel. How cornered.

Remember how I said that social media and smartphones *desensitize* us? How technology makes us act in ways that we would never act in person? How it teaches us that other people are objects? How it actually creates *distance* between what we post and the person behind the post? How it makes us act in ways that are much less human and that devalue others and others' feelings and bodies?

Well. Here is a perfect example of this.

My point here is *not* to make you feel guilty or ashamed of sexting because, as you know, I am not a big fan of guilt and shame. I am not saying that *all* sexting is bad. But I *am* a fan of doing serious thinking about our behavior and sexting requires some of this.

The college students I interviewed for my research were about fifty/fifty in how they felt about sexting. Some were into it and some were not.

One guy even outlined for me what he called "the ethics of sexting"! He said that sending sexy pictures and texts was okay within a relationship, especially a long-distance one. (A lot of the pro-sexting people echoed this opinion.) But sexting should only occur with someone you trusted and with whom you had real intimacy. He also told me that sexting was only a good idea if you *both* sent each other pictures and sexy texts because this guaranteed "mutually assured destruction," as he put it.

Most of this sounded reasonably okay.

But that last bit makes me concerned: that sexting could put you in a position to *destroy* another person if you wanted, and vice versa; that this destruction could occur by one of the two parties deciding to send those intimate photos and comments to countless other people or post them online for all the world to see (and see forever). That's how powerful sexts are. *So* powerful that you could actually really hurt, even "destroy," that other person, and in so many different ways.

Sexts, possessing sexts and sexy photos of someone else, gives a person *a lot* of power. You suddenly hold in your hand, literally, the power to humiliate and shame that person, to take something incredibly intimate and share it with others who have no business seeing it (an entire *world* of others), to cruelly and heartlessly violate their privacy in a way that can never be taken back and can risk their reputation for a lifetime to come. The repercussions of sharing someone's sexts are so enormous that it's difficult to conceive of how enormous they might get (and this is part of the problem—often, those people who *do* share sexts don't think about the possible consequences before doing so). Not to mention, doing so potentially has criminal repercussions.

I hope all of this bothers you a bit.

This is where I need you to be a thinking *human* and remember that there is *always* another human on the other end of your texts. And before you make a request of someone—or respond to a request from someone else—I really, *really* want you to think before you do anything.

Ask yourself:

* Does this request—or my response to this request—fit with my relational ethic?

* Does this request—or my response to this request—respect this person as a fellow, feeling human being?

* Would I do this—or respond to this—if it was happening in person and not over text? If I was standing in front of the person, physically, in real time, one human body to another human body?

* Have I taken into consideration the possible consequences, for all parties involved, of making or responding to this request?

If you've answered *no* to any of these questions, I think you have a lot more thinking to do before you hit *send*.

Social Media, Smartphones, Care, and Consent

I've been talking a lot about *care* and *ethics*.

How I want you to be caring people. How I want you to be ethical people, especially when it comes to your relationships and to sex. Well, I want you to be caring, ethical people on social media and on your smartphones when you text, too.

If you are an aspiring good, compassionate, caring friend and romantic partner to others, I don't want you to suddenly forget all that when you grab for your phone. I don't want you to turn into someone who texts mean things or who requests boob pics from some vulnerable person you don't even know very well at school—or from someone you do know pretty well either. (Save a few sexy things for later, wouldya?) I don't want you to be this generally good person who suddenly changes to not so good when a bunch of people are around you, looking at your phone, and egging you on to do something that rattles your conscience.

Just because we can't see someone's reaction doesn't mean we haven't had an effect on them. And the ways you act toward others? Those always, always, *always* produce an effect. Even if it's via social media and on text. There is no getting out of this. You may not see it, but that doesn't mean it isn't there. It doesn't mean you didn't hurt or shame someone.

The presence of social media and smartphones and the screens they place between us can shift us away from the selves we'd like to be. They can encourage us to act in ways that don't feel right to us, that make us uncomfortable, that make us feel unhealthy.

A Big Question I asked earlier: *What does it mean to have a healthy relationship with social media and our smartphones?* It's a Big Question because it doesn't have an easy answer. Right now, our entire culture is engaged in asking it (or at least, we should be) because none of us are quite sure what a healthy relationship looks like. The earlier *you* get asking this question, the better off you will be.

Social media and smartphones pose Big Challenges to how we understand ourselves and what it means to be human. They are encouraging us to see our humanity, to see other humans, in some rather *in*human ways. As we learn to "sell ourselves" effectively online, one of the things that becomes less important is our *hearts*—and the hearts of others. Social media and smartphones are desensitizing us to so much of who we really are and who we need to be in order to foster good, healthy, ethical, and consensual relationships with others.

Humanity, vulnerability, intimacy, ethics, care, and consent are connected.

Being a sexual being—one who cares about consent and living out and up to our sexual ethic—requires us to be at our *most* human. It requires us to respect and value our own body and the bodies of others. The more distanced we are from our physical selves and from the feelings of others, the more difficult it is for us to grasp the meaning and purpose of sex, and the dignity and worth of our partners and our partners' bodies. It becomes easy to shrug off what we cannot see and to shrug off our responsibility for the feelings of others.

We are working so hard to try and pretend like everything is okay, even great, all the time; that nothing can affect us, that we can walk away from relationships or comments or hurtful actions with a shrug any time we want, without a scratch. But for the vast majority of us, somewhere deep down—we *do* care.

So how can we break this cycle of performance?

Time To Do a Social Media Personal Inventory:

Do you have an Online You versus a Real You? If the answer is yes, spend some time describing one version of you, and then the other one. What are the differences between these two yous? Where are the similarities? Is there one "you" that you like better? If so, why? Make a list of reasons.

Now take an inventory of the feelings you experience while you are online. Does being on your social media accounts make you feel good or less than good? When do you feel positive and when do you feel not so positive? Are there certain platforms that make you feel better than others? Like, do you like Snapchat better than Instagram? Instagram better than Facebook? If there is one platform you prefer above all others, consider prioritizing that account above the others, or even deleting those other apps from your phone, to try to maximize your health and well-being when you are scrolling.

Pick at least one post that made you feel good about yourself and/or others or the world. Try to understand *why* it made you feel good. Now do the opposite. Pick a post or photo that made you feel not so good. Try to understand why it made you feel bad. Keep these things in mind as you go online in the future—these criteria can help you sort through what to focus on and what to avoid.

Next, I want you to pick a conversation that happened over text that makes you feel unsettled, maybe not so good, maybe a bit uncomfortable or even unsafe. I want you to spend some time thinking about *why.* What is it about this text conversation that unsettles you? Is it something you said that you don't feel good about? Is it something someone else said to you that makes you feel upset or bad about yourself?

Finally, take out your relational ethic. I want you to look at it, and ask yourself: What does it mean to be a good friend over text? What does it mean to be a good friend over social media? And I want you to explore the opposite, too: What does it mean to be a *not-so-good* friend over text and social media?

Why Do We Perform So Much for Others?

Technically, We Don't Live in a Theater!

Have you ever been in a musical or a play?

It's fun to act, to become another person, to slip on someone else's life like you might put on a coat. To try on all sorts of ways of being that are not normally you. When we act in a play we can take risks, do dangerous things, scream and yell and cry, all without consequences! And then people applaud. Woohoo!

But we are actresses and actors in our daily lives, too. We try on all kinds of roles, sometimes many different roles in a single day. We are constantly performing.

All of us do it. Absolutely all of us. Me included. No one is exempt.

Just think about one of the first things you do every day

before you go to school: you decide what you're going to wear. You stand in front of your closet and think about what sort of image you want to give people. Maybe you dress like a model, maybe you dress like a jock, maybe you pick out an outfit totally designed to impress that person you have a crush on, maybe you dye your hair a different color every month, or maybe you wear all black clothing, all the time. When we think about how we want to look, we will dress to please ourselves, but we will often be thinking about how other people perceive us. It's a rare person who truly doesn't care what other people think.

It's totally normal to care what other people think!

I care. You care. We all do.

We are performing all the time. Sometimes it's for our parents or even our grandparents. You act differently around grandma than you do around your friends, right? Sometimes it's for a certain group of people at school that we want to notice us. Sometimes it's for our teachers or our coaches. We have ideas about what we want other people to think of us and we act accordingly. There are an infinite number of *audiences* out there and we are like chameleons, changing our spots depending on the scenery. We are really good at what we do!

And sometimes, we *really* want to change how people perceive us.

Ever had a makeover? A time when you've tried to change your look, your life, your social standing at school? Who your friends are or how well you do academically or whether or not you are an athlete or the *star* athlete on a team? Sometimes we try to lose weight or bulk up our muscle or transform our hairstyle or go from shy and quiet and not so noticeable to energetic and boisterous and impossible *not* to notice.

Especially as we grow up, we experiment with who we are.

Experimentation is great. It can be empowering and fun and informative. We learn a lot about ourselves, what works for us, what doesn't, when we play around with our personalities and try on new roles. Experimenting with who we are, how we act, what we look like, how we dress, can be a healthy and fun. It can help us to figure out who we really are and how we want to be. Which is *awesome*.

But this kind of performing can also become toxic.

(Yes, *toxic* is another of those words I bring up a lot, like when I've talked about gossip. Let's unpack it here.)

A toxin is a kind of poison, something that is not good for us, that can even be lethal. At a certain level, performing for others can become poisonous. Performing can become especially poisonous when we are dealing with things in our lives that make us feel insecure or that don't have easy answers.

Let's take *popularity*.

Whether or not we are considered popular at school can lead us to do a lot of performing. Sometimes our attempts to conform to what counts as popular can become destructive. They can turn us into people who are mean to others and make us behave in ways that we *know* go completely against our relational ethic (like with social media).

There is a point where our performances for various audiences at school and on social media and over text and in our social lives in general can begin to take over who we are. So many of the students I meet complain that, by the time they get to college, so much acting is expected of them to fulfill all the (often toxic) norms they face, that the person they really believe they are, the *self* they wish they could be, gets buried so far down that they never let this person out in the open again. This makes them frustrated, sad, and lonely. Too much performing can make us feel alienated from ourselves and from everyone around us.

As opposed to that good kind of experimentation, that helps us *discover* ourselves even more, and that brings out the best and the new that was hiding inside of us.

I've already talked about how guys learn to perform guy-ness, how people learn to perform shrugs in the face of someone they really care about, how everyone is trying so hard to perform happiness on social media. But now, we're honing in on performance in general, because stereotypes and expectations that others have set can force us into performing roles we never wanted to play. And if *you* are going to be doing any performing, I want it to be the kind that lets you experiment with who you are and not the kind that makes you feel *less* you, or might even be *destructive* to the you that you are.

Facing a Culture of Performance: Shoulda, Have-ta, Aren't Allowed-ta

A couple of years ago on a visit to a small liberal arts college, a group of students invited me to have dinner with them. They were an official student group, dedicated to meeting every week to talk about sex and relationships. We filled our plates with food and then formed a big circle. There were about twenty-five of us. As we ate, people reflected on the talk I'd just given that evening about sex on college campuses. Our conversation meandered all over the place until it eventually got to an extended discussion of one issue in particular:

Kissing on the dance floor.

"Remember when you could just make out on the dance floor?" one student said.

A number of other people chimed in their agreement, reminiscing about all those times back in high school when they were "allowed to" just kiss each other while dancing at a party or, well, at a dance.

"Why can't you kiss on the dance floor now?" I asked.

The students went on to explain the following:

"You're only allowed to do that in high school. When you get to college, you're no longer supposed to do that. In college you 'have to' hook up and have sex. That's just the deal."

"Who says?" I asked next.

"I don't know," was their vague response. "This is just the way college is."

"Yes, but who *decided* this is the way college is?" I pressed.

There was a lot of shrugging. "It's just what everybody knows," they said.

Now the students went on to explain what they believed was expected of them (sexually) at college—expectations that got in the way of them getting to "just kiss on the dance floor." It involved a lot of role-playing and script-following on their parts. Performing, in other words.

At parties and wherever there was dancing, sure there might be kissing during the dancing, but there couldn't be *only* kissing. If there *was* kissing, the guy was expected to invite the girl (because this was a heterosexual situation) back to his room where they'd be expected to hook up—even if they didn't want to, were too tired, were not in the mood to. So, this exhausted, post-dancing couple goes back to someone's room and proceeds to do the hooking up and spends most of the time looking forward to the hookup being over so everybody can go home to bed if they aren't home already. And how do you know it's okay to end the hookup so people can do what they really want, which is to sleep?

"You know the hookup is over when the guy comes," one of the young women explained.

"Yeah," said another. "You gotta make the guy come or you can't go home yet."

The guys in the room complained how difficult it was to come when they were really tired and not so sober, and the girls complained how difficult it was to make a guy come when everybody was really tired and not so sober.

"What about trying to make the girl come, too?" I asked.

"That wasn't really feasible," they explained. After all, everybody is exhausted, probably a little bit drunk, and they don't really want to be doing what they're doing in the first place. To pile the girl's orgasm on top of the guy's was just too much.

I pushed the students to think about all of these expectations again. Who set them? Who made them up? Who was requiring men and women to play these predetermined roles, to perform these expectations—expectations that were so decentering to what everyone really wanted to do, which again was pretty simple: make out on the dance floor. I also pointed out all those "shoulds," "have-tos," and "musts" I heard in their story.

The upshot?

This group of students and so many others I've met are *performing* a set of expectations around sex that they don't necessarily like or agree with, nor do they even know who *authored* these expectations. (The God of College Sex?) Even though this group of students knew what they wanted to do and thought would be fun—just kissing on the dance floor—they felt so pressured to conform to outside expectations (to play the role of "normal college student around sex") that they ended up *performing* a hookup. And in this case, the performing was not the good kind that is experimentation, but the alienating kind rooted in a need to *conform*. Many students feel cornered into this kind of sexual encounter, like they don't have any other option aside from *playing out a predetermined set of roles and scripts*.

I Want You to Play! . . . But Not Like That

Like I said, experimentation is a good thing.

Play is a good thing.

Playing around with roles and scripts can be really fun, too.

Sometimes playing around with roles and scripts and experimenting can be really liberating. It can *empower* us to try on experiences, relationships, identities that we wouldn't otherwise have the guts to try on. But when our performing is really about *conforming*, when our performing is about feeling like we have *no other choice* but to behave in a certain way, this is not empowering at all.

If you find yourself or one of your friends trying to justify behavior that doesn't feel quite right to you, with rationales like:

This is just the way it is.
That's just what people do in high school . . . in college . . .
wherever.
We should . . . We've gotta . . . You just have-ta . . .

I want you to pause a moment and ask yourself:

What is the source of this rule? Does it come from an identifiable and trustworthy source? Like a good friend, a teacher, your parents, your religious community, a family member, a philosopher, a novelist, or someone similar that you think is super-smart and has your best interests at heart? Or is the source impossible to identify?

Like, um . . . is it the God of High School Sex?

Or just . . . people? Vague, unidentifiable people?

Amorphous "wes" and "theys" that don't have faces?

And does this unidentifiable source have very specific

expectations for men as opposed to women? For LGBTQ people as opposed to heterosexual people? For what's supposed to happen versus what isn't versus what you are supposed to feel and do versus what you aren't? What is "normal" versus what is "abnormal"?

Finally, I want you to ask yourself: Is this thing that I'm doing, or about to do, or expected to do—does it really feel like *me*? Does it thrill me, feel daring in a good way, draw out a new side of me that is kind of cool and weird and I like it? Does it teach me new things about myself that are good to know?

If the answer is no?

Then whatever it is you've gotta, have-ta, supposed-ta do is probably not the empowering kind of playful performance. It's probably not of the good-experimentation kind. And I want you to be strong enough to A) realize this and B) resist feeling pressured into performing whatever it is. That's not the fun kind of theater. And the theater is supposed to be fun.

So How Do *You* Perform?

Make a list of ways that you "perform" for people at school. Start with how you dress and why, and continue on with any and all roles you can think of: athlete, theater person, nonconformist rebel, popular girl, band geek, the good student. Describe all the things required of you to perform that role effectively. Make a list of *groups of people* that you perform for, in specific ways, and describe what each group or person requires of you that is different.

Now ask yourself: How do these roles make you feel? Does playing certain roles make you feel better than others? If so, why do you think that is? Are there any roles you perform that make you feel *really far away* from the person you want to be or who you think you really are? Are there any roles you'd like to give up performing? And if so, what would it take for you to let go of them?

What if you were to do a makeover, in the hopes of figuring out how to "play" the role of the person you *truly* are. So much of this book is about becoming a critical thinker about yourself—and I want you to spend some time, right now, thinking about how you might be able to bring the roles you play into close contact with that person you know, deep inside, that you really are. I want you to try to figure out how to perform your true self! In the most authentic way you can come up with!

What do you think would happen if you were more honest about yourself and who you really are and what you really wish for? What are you most afraid of happening? What might you gain from trying this? What do you stand to lose if you don't?

Just think on this.

What Is Hookup Culture? (And Why Is It Problematic?)

Hooking Up: Theory Versus Reality

For years and years, I've been talking to students about hooking up on college campuses. The reason? When I first started my research, when I would ask people about sex, they would respond by talking about hooking up. It became clear that we couldn't have a conversation about sex without also talking about hookups and hookup culture. Which means that we need to talk about it here, too.

Hookups have become one of those norms people feel pressure to perform and live up to—even if it's not their thing. The scripts and roles for sexual intimacy and attitudes for one's partners that hookup culture sets are the kind that discourage care, vulnerability, connection, and communication—and,

207

because of this, consent. A culture of hooking up discourages, even *devalues*, many of the kinds of things that should ground and shape a person's relational and sexual ethics.

I defined this practice briefly earlier, but I'll define it more fully now:

THE HOOKUP:

* It's brief. Maybe five minutes brief, maybe an entire night.

* There's sexual activity. Anything from kissing to sexual intercourse.

* Don't get attached. You walk away afterward like the whole thing and your partner with it was one big shrug. Whatever.

* Alcohol. (This one is unofficial, but pretty typical.)

In *theory*, the hookup is supposed to be about liberation from commitment and basically from 1950s ideas (and religious prohibitions) around sex. It's meant to put the "casual" into "casual sex." You meet someone, have an amazing encounter, and walk away sexually satisfied, all without the fuss of a relationship and even if you never talk to that person again. In *theory*, it sounds great.

Woohoo!

Most of the college students I speak with want to hang on to their *right* to hook up. I am in favor of options when it comes to sex, so the hookup being one option out of many for sexual intimacy sounds fine, in theory.

But . . .

The hookup in *reality*—the real, lived experiences that college students report about hooking up—is something altogether different. The vast majority of students do not experience hookups as liberating.

In my initial research, the happiest hookups had students saying hookups were "fine." As in, "just *fine.*" As in, just kinda okay? The middle group said "whatever" about them. As in, hookups are, you know, *whatever.* Not great, not horrible, just . . . huh. Shrug-worthy. Something that you just do because "that's what people do in college." Like, go to soccer practice, study at the library, do the dishes, get the hookup done. The last group of students told terrible stories about hooking up, some of which involved sexual violence. As in, their experiences of hookups were horrible.

So where were all the amazing hookups? The super fun ones? Hooking up was supposed to be the pinnacle of sexual liberation, but the ways students were describing their hookups didn't seem liberating at all.

Performing the Hookup

I know by now you know a lot about *performance.* And well, hookup culture is a culture of pretend.

College students are great pretenders when it comes to their hookups. Everybody knows it is *supposed to* be amazing. That it's *supposed to* be super fun. That it's supposed to *prove* you are sexually liberated. (Here come the "supposed tos" again.) In public, people's stories about hooking up become quite the *performance* of awesomeness.

But in private, students tell you those not-so-great, even seriously depressing stories about the realities of their experience. Which amount to either *hookups are blah* or *hookups really kinda suck*. And though almost everyone wants to hang onto their *right* to hook up (their choice to do so), the thing that really frustrates people is feeling stuck, living in a *culture* of hooking up.

In a *culture* of hooking up, the hookup becomes the dominant framework for sexual intimacy (whether it's kissing or a variety of types of sexual intercourse). The hookup becomes the dominant *gateway* to sexual intimacy. So, rather than the hookup being one option *among many* for sexual intimacy, people see it as *the only option* for sexual encounters with new partners. Everything has to go *through* the hookup, including the committed relationships that eventually may come out of that first hookup, even though (in theory) relationships aren't *supposed to* result from hookups.

A culture of hooking up affects everyone, regardless of sexual orientation and gender identity. But for LGBTQ students, this culture has its own implications. LGBTQ students will often say that because the pool of potential partners on campus is smaller than the pool for heterosexual students, often by a lot (that is, there simply aren't as many LGBTQ students as heterosexual students), that makes hookup culture more prone to gossip. Everyone knows who is hooking up with whom because there are fewer potential partners, and this causes lots of drama (and heartbreak) within the LGBTQ community, and can lead to a lot of slut-shaming, too.

Also, there is a cultural myth floating around that during college all women at some point hook up with other women. I even went to one campus where a first-year all-women's hall was dubbed the "virgin vault" in September, the "slut hut" by December, followed by the "lesbian lair" by spring semester. Because of assumptions like these, women who identify as lesbian—as "real lesbians" as some of them put it—sometimes feel the need to *prove themselves* as lesbians. This puts pressure on them to engage in hookups they may not really want to engage in as a kind of proof, and injects mistrust about people's sexual identity.

Regardless of how a person identifies, a culture of hooking up *closes off* choice, and it tends to *silence* people's voices. In order to *conform* to its pressures, people end up hiding what they really feel. They *perform* the role of how they believe they are *supposed to* feel and act. And everyone tries to do their best to act like they don't care about sex or their partners—engaging in that competition to see "who cares the least," and whoever cares the least wins the game, as those students told me over pizza.

The problem is that nobody really wins this game that is hookup culture. A culture of hooking up forces certain roles and scripts onto everybody (like parts in a play that you didn't want to be in), which causes people to act in ways that don't reflect their real beliefs and feelings about sex and their partners.

As you know by now, this kind of performing is *not* good. And it's particularly problematic for consent.

Hookup Culture and Consent: A Paradox

Journalists are always asking if I'm against hookups and hookup culture.

I used to say *no*, I'm not against hooking up. And, in *theory*, I'm not, in the sense that if two people want to engage in sexual intimacy that is mutual and respectful over the course of a single evening and part ways the next day, I really do think that's fine.

The thing is, that's not what hookups-in-*reality* look like. This is *not* how hookups tend to play out for people on the ground. Hookups in the context of hookup culture often leave the "mutual and respectful" part of the sexual intimacy out.

So nowadays, when people ask me if I'm anti–hooking up, I've stopped saying I'm okay with it because I now know that hookup culture sells people a lie about sexual liberation; it coerces people into performing roles and scripts they do not like or agree with, and discourages the *care* toward the well-being of one's partner that consent requires.

So, yup. I'm anti–hookup culture. There. I said it.

I'm not a fan of being anti-anything with respect to sex. (I hope you've figured that out by now.) But I have to draw the line with a culture that instills some of the most problematic values about sex I've ever seen—values, or *anti-values*, that enable and perpetuate sexual violence, and that lead to sexual *disempowerment*. Feminism, as I said earlier, is about choice, voice, access and options, and justice, and hookup culture tends to actively thwart these very things, which makes a culture of hooking up *anti-feminist*, too.

The story that hookup culture passes on about sex—and that will likely get passed on to you—is a story that, at its heart, promotes an *anti-ethic* about sex.

Hookup Culture's Anti-Sexual Ethic

I know. You just spent all this time coming up with your own sexual ethic and here comes an entire culture that likely goes against everything you stand for about sex and relationships.

Maybe you are contending with hookup culture already among your friends and at school. Or maybe someone will repackage it with a new and shinier name by the time you get to college (or they have already). I want you to be ready for when you *do* encounter it, whatever it's called. I want you to be prepared with a good sense of *your* sexual ethic, so you can measure yours against hookup culture's anti-ethic.

So what do I mean by an "anti-ethic"?

A culture of hooking up passes down the story (or the script) that sex is supposed to be casual and that your partner doesn't have to matter. As in, sex is casual so don't make it a big deal and you can use your partner kind of like they're a plastic sex toy. Hookup culture passes down the story that it is normal, even expected, to *objectify* our partners. (And we've already talked about the problems with objectification—objectification diminishes and even denies our humanity.)

The story hookup culture sells is that sex happens *outside* of relational and sexual ethics.

As in, it's a-ethical (outside of). It doesn't have to concern itself with ethics.

But this doesn't work. Its premise is *false*.

Any time you are dealing with sex, especially if you're having sex with another person, you are wading into the territory of ethics—sexual ethics, in particular. You already know this. Relationships, all of them, every single one, are ethical in nature. They involve more than one person, they involve people interacting, and therefore they operate within ethical parameters. That's just how ethics works. All communities are ethical bodies and all communal occurrences have ethical significance attached to them. You are engaging in behaviors that have ethical implications all day, all the time. You've been doing it your entire life. Because most of us are in the presence of others constantly.

More than one person = ethical situation.
One person + another person = ethical situation.
Becoming sexually intimate with someone = ethical situation.

There isn't any getting out of this. You can try and *pretend* that sexual intimacy can happen *apart from* ethics, but if you do, you are performing a *lie*. Performing that lie can get people into real problems with regard to consent. This is one of the big reasons relational and sexual ethics are so important.

Your relational and sexual ethic can help *correct* the story (the lie) that hookup culture might try and sell to you about sex and your partners. You can use your own ethic to measure against any outside ethic, including if it's an "anti-ethic."

Let's take one of the central "teachings" that hookup culture passes on:

My sexual partner is an object there for my own personal use and self-gratification.

Now ask yourself:

How does this "teaching" measure against my relational and sexual ethics? How does it honor or dishonor my understanding of good friends and good partners?

If you have found that *using* others and having others *use* you (objectification) doesn't fit your relational ethic, then your response to the teaching *My sexual partner is an object there for my own personal use and self-gratification* should be one of serious caution. If it doesn't feel like it fits, if it makes you fidget, then take a step back and think about it more and, ideally, discuss it.

The great thing about having your own sexual ethic, especially one that is flexible enough to change and expand as you get older and as your relationships and partners change, and your ideas about sex do too, is that it's *useful* in the face of *any* framework for sexual ethics that you encounter in your community, in other people, in the world around you as you move through it.

You have the authority and power and right to measure your own ethic against an ethic you inherit, or that someone is trying to convince you is the right thing.

Sometimes you might find that the new teaching or script offered to you is great! Or has some great ideas or options you'd like to include in your own sexual ethic. But if the teaching or the script is not so great, then you'll have some hard decisions to make. Especially if everyone else around you is pretending that this stuff is okay (you know, treating their partners like plastic sex toys).

It's your *right* to consult your sexual ethic. (Your trusty compass.)

It's also your *responsibility* to do this.

That's why you built it in the first place.

Your Hookup Homework:

Spend some time writing down anything you've ever learned about hooking up and hookup culture—if anything. Or if you recognize some of the ideas you've inherited about sex in what I've described here as a culture of hooking up. Spend some time reflecting on this and pondering what you think of hookup culture.

The other best thing you can do is do read some more about hookup culture. I want you to be informed! Information is empowering—it really is.

ADVICE TO OUR YOUNGER SELVES PART III

"Dear 12-year-old-self: No one has told you this yet, but sexuality is not a linear or solid thing. Liking a boy, or liking a girl, will not change or define who you are. Who you are will change again and again over the course of your life, with each person you meet and each time you fall in and out of love. Do not be afraid to change, and do not let fear of labels hold you back from pursuing something new and scary and exciting. Sexuality is fluid; embrace the uncertainty that comes with love and desire, and never be so afraid of the unknown that you miss out on something—or someone—great."
                  —BRIANA MACDONALD, author of *Pepper's Rules for*
                  Secret Sleuthing

"Adam, right now, you are obsessed with girls. You want to be with them so much you think you might explode. And yet you can't bring yourself to tell them. You are friends with them, you listen to them, share just a little (just what you want them to hear, no more), but you never tell them that you would love to kiss them, if only you were brave enough to be honest. And that is okay. It really is. It doesn't feel okay, because you are worried you are going to spontaneously combust from desire and leave bloody pulp all over the walls. But you won't. And when you're ready, you will tell them. And when you're older, you will think back to this time and try to remember what it was like to feel *anything* this intensely. It's a unique moment in your life. The pain will pass. You'll kiss them when you're ready. And when the girl makes it clear that she is ready. You really do care about these girls. That's the important thing. The pain will be a memory . . . eventually, a good one. Eventually, one that might even make you laugh. Eventually. You can do it. Love, Old Adam."

–ADAM GIDWITZ, author of *The Inquisitor's Tale* and
The Unicorn Rescue Society

"If I could go back in time, I'd gently explain to myself that there's a huge difference between *wanting to* and *willing to* when it comes to evaluating a potential sexual encounter. My self-esteem was so rotten back then, I never once stopped to evaluate *my* interest in the boys who showed interest in me. Instead, I viewed their overtures as some sort of lucky opportunity that happened to fall in my lap, a chance that I couldn't or shouldn't pass up."

–SIOBHAN VIVIAN, author of *We Are the Wildcats* and *The List*

"Hey, twelve-year-old Darcie. Adult Darcie here. It's time for 'the talk.' Look, I know sex is the last thing on your mind. In fact, it's still the last thing on your mind. And that's totally fine! Just keep being you. You're gonna have a lot of adventures. You'll research plankton in the Sargasso Sea. Visit a thousand haunted houses. Fall in love. Win fights that matter. Read many, many, MANY wonderful books. I'm not claiming your life will be perfect. Trust me, you'll know more heartbreak, anger and hardship. That said, the beauty and joy in your life will outweigh the bad. It'll be okay. Really. And you sure as hell don't need sex to be a happy, mature, mostly-got-your-shit-together grown-up. But you already suspect that, don't you?"

–DARCIE LITTLE BADGER, author of *Elatsoe*

"Güero, your parents—mine, ours—mess up all the time. Still, they've taught us something essential, an enduring truth: we're all equal, regardless of gender, none subject to the will of another. You've already found that girls make amazing friends, and in time you'll begin to date—girls and boys and all those rainbowed souls in between. Remember that each of them has full rights over their body. You'll ache for their warmth, their touch. But always ask. Desire's not enough. You need their consent. I promise you: that smiling 'yes' is the most beautiful thing in the world."

—DAVID BOWLES, author of *Feathered Serpent, Dark Heart of Sky* and *They Call Me Güero*

"I wish that I could tell my 12-year-old disabled self that even though it isn't easy to be disabled, your body and mind have value. It's okay to be disabled, and one day you will make decisions about your sex life and your body that people will look up to. I would tell my 12 year old disabled self that consent for disabled people is so much more layered than simply yes or no; there is a whole lot of trust that disabled people have to put into sexual decisions, and I would tell my teenaged disabled self not to worry so much about what able-bodied people thought about you or your disability, and just enjoy being the weird, quirky disabled guy you are inside."

—ANDREW GURZA, Disability Awareness Consultant

PART THREE

Consent

What Is Sexual Violence?

The #MeToo Movement and What It Says About Our World

Unless you've been living under a rock or down at the South Pole among the penguins, you probably know something about #MeToo. You've either seen that hashtag on Twitter, Instagram, or Facebook, you've heard about it in the news, or maybe someone close to you has claimed #MeToo themselves. Maybe *you've* even claimed it.

In 2006, activist Tarana Burke began using the phrase "Me Too" to provide the space and opportunity for women of color to speak and come together around the issue of sexual abuse. Burke wanted to encourage women to voice their experiences of assault and abuse and to know they aren't alone.

Then in October 2017, following multiple accusations of sexual assault against the media mogul Harvey Weinstein by Hollywood actresses, suddenly the hashtag #MeToo was everywhere.

The actress Alyssa Milano, in solidarity with Weinstein's victims and victims of sexual violence everywhere, encouraged people to use the hashtag #MeToo to voice their own experiences of violence and harassment.

Soon #MeToo was absolutely *everywhere*.

Women of all backgrounds, ages, and professions, in countries all over the world publicly claimed #MeToo. Many of these claims took down some of the most powerful men in the entertainment industry and in politics, too, from Matt Lauer, the host of the *Today* show, to the comedian Louis C.K., to Al Franken, a US senator from Minnesota. Women tweeted and Instagrammed and Facebooked stories of sexual assault that ranged from unwanted kissing to rape at gunpoint. Women spoke out about the unwanted comments they were forced to endure by bosses and coworkers, unwanted attention, unwanted flirtation, unwanted everything you can imagine.

The sheer number of women (and some men) who have spoken on behalf of so much unwanted and violent experience stunned the public. It has also raised awareness about how sexual violence and harassment are an insidious reality for nearly all girls and women during their lifetimes. The #MeToo movement has offered people an opportunity and space to be public about their experiences of sexual assault and harassment. It's given people a voice and solidarity.

So #MeToo has been incredibly telling for our world.

But what does it tell us, exactly?

The #MeToo movement has shown us a lot about the world we live in, and how it values—or *devalues*—girls, women, and female bodies. It has shown us how much violence and harass-ment girls and women face as they live and move about in our world, and the fact that sexual violence and harassment is *a nor-mal part* of what it means to be a girl and a woman in our world. It has revealed how pervasive a problem sexual violence and harassment is in our schools, our lives, our workplaces, and it has shown us exactly how much work we have to do to contend with sexual violence and harassment prevention—a lot. We're talking, WOW, a lot.

So, #MeToo is empowering and vindicating for victims.

But #MeToo is terrible news because of how it reveals the widespread lack of respect and regard our world has for half its population, and how far we have to go to contend with sexual violence and harassment. Really far. Like, super, super far.

Sexual Violence: The Opposite of Consent

When I was in college, people mainly thought of sexual violence in terms of the rapist who jumps out of the bushes in the middle of the night, holding a gun or a knife. Sexual assault was some-thing perpetrated by a stranger, a violent criminal in a dark alley.

That doesn't fit the reality of most sexual violence.

Sexual violence is usually perpetrated by someone you know, maybe even someone you know well, whom you trust, even someone with whom you are in a romantic relationship (intimate-partner violence). More likely than not, you already know someone who is the victim of sexual violence, or maybe even you, yourself, are a victim. Maybe this is why the hashtag #MeToo is familiar to you. Statistics vary, but generally between 20–25 percent of college women experience some form of sexual violence before they graduate. Think about that—between one in four or one in five college women are the victims of assault. Did you know that one of the things that puts women at risk of sexual violence is *going to college*?

Yeah. That's the truth.

So what *is* sexual violence?

Basically, it's any unwanted sexual contact. This could range from an unwanted kiss to unwanted touching, to nonconsensual sexual intercourse.

Sexual assault is *not* defined by whether or not the assaulter has a weapon, or whether or not the victim fights back or screams and kicks, or whether the victim is wearing lots of makeup or a short skirt. Sometimes the person committing the sexual violence has no idea they are committing violence against another person—but this doesn't mean that they *didn't* commit the violence. Perpetrators convince themselves of all sorts of things, like that their victims "wanted" it, that somehow having sex with someone against their will or while they are physically unable to consent is a "normal" and understandable thing to do.

What is sexual harassment?

It's any unwanted attention, commentary, gestures, actions of a sexual nature toward another person.

Even though sexual violence and harassment—unwanted sexual contact and attention—sound pretty simple, definition-wise, it is anything but simple to claim oneself as a victim, and to hold the perpetrator accountable. Biases in society and culture about the very things I listed above—what a victim is wearing, whether or not they fight back, if they are known to be flirts, if perhaps they really "wanted it" after all, especially if they know the assaulter or the harasser—become an enormous mountain that most victims of assault and harassment simply do not want to scale. The odds of getting justice are stacked against victims and very much favor the perpetrator. It's difficult to prove sexual assault in particular, often because it is one person's word against another, and there are typically few witnesses if any.

This is another reason #MeToo has been so important. Because it is *so* difficult to get justice, many women have decided to turn to the "court of public opinion" in an effort to hold their assaulters and harassers accountable. Either the legal system, their workplaces, or their schools *already failed* them in this regard, or they felt that they simply had no outlet for justice. This aspect of #MeToo has been controversial because it sidesteps the legal system and the policies schools and workplaces have in place to deal with such claims. But the belief goes that these laws and policies favor the perpetrator, the company, and the institution over the victim, and that #MeToo has helped to right this balance.

I would *like* to say that things are changing for the better on the victims-gaining-justice front, but I'm not sure this is actually true. Social and legal gains have been made in the last fifteen years for victims, but ongoing news stories about sexual assault cases that are moving through the courts tend to prove exactly how difficult it is for victims to find justice.

We only need to look to the White House for evidence of the *lack* of justice. President Donald Trump has been accused of assaulting more than fifteen women, and yet, he was elected. This sends a message to all victims of sexual violence and perpetrators, too—that victims will likely not see justice, and perpetrators who get away with committing this kind of violence may even be celebrated and promoted as a result. The election of Donald Trump is part of what sparked the #MeToo movement. Women were fed up with this message that no one really cares about how, to be a girl and a woman in our culture, is to be made a victim.

The Many Ways We Silence and Blame the Victim

A minute ago, I suggested that you likely know a victim of sexual violence. But maybe you can't name anyone. Maybe you are scratching your head and thinking, What in the world is she talking about? Or simply—not *me*, I don't know anybody. Not even with people claiming #MeToo all over the place!

But chances are, you really *do* know someone. It may be someone close to you, like a parent, an aunt, a grandparent. It may be one of your best friends. Or it may be someone more distant, like an acquaintance at school, a teacher, a coach, a neighbor, a family friend.

So why can't you name that person?

Most victims of sexual violence do not come forward—ever. This has been changing, lately, because of #MeToo. But many victims keep what happened to them silent for months, years, even decades, not telling another soul, not even the people who love them most. It is common for victims of sexual violence to not speak up or out—*ever*.

There are many, many possible reasons for their silence. Among them are:

* Knowing that the perpetrator is not likely to be held accountable.

* They feel ashamed of what happened, or worry that it might be their fault because they didn't fight back or should have somehow prevented their own assault or harassment—and worry that others will feel this way, too.

* They fear that no one will believe them—because our society has a long history of not believing women.

* They fear the perpetrator.

* They fear the larger social, professional, and relational repercussions and backlash.

Many victims worry (rightly) about the stigma that will be attached to them if they attempt to seek justice against a perpetrator. There are many cases on college campuses where students came forward to report an assault and then had to transfer out of their school because people didn't believe them and were angry they would dare try and "ruin" the life of the perpetrator (among other possible responses).

Our society and culture have long followed a blame-the-victim model for responding to victims of sexual assault and harassment. This is why victims associate coming forward with risking being "victimized twice"—the first time during the assault, the second during the assault on one's character and life that occurs if a victim seeks justice.

On some campuses, rather than show concern for victims, schools will advocate for the perpetrator, especially if he is an important athlete. Colleges and universities have been silencing victims and stories of assault committed by important athletes on campus for decades.

Taken together, these circumstances make it very difficult for a victim to come forward and seek justice against a perpetrator. Likewise, they can make it very difficult for a victim to speak at all, to tell someone, anyone, even a trusted confidant. The thought sometimes goes that it is "easier" for a victim to try and put what happened behind them, to move forward with their life, as though the assault didn't happen at all.

The Ups and Downs of Title IX and Sexual Violence

You might know about Title IX if you are a girl and you play a sport. Title IX is the 1972 federal law that famously empowered my generation of girls to become a generation of athletes. It mandates equal access to sports for women. If boys have a certain number of teams, players, scholarships, then girls have to get an equivalent number, too. Yahoo!

But Title IX has always been about more than sports. It's also about equal access, treatment, and rights in relation to sex and gender, and about preventing gender discrimination, too.

In April 2011, the Obama administration sent a letter to all colleges and universities in the United States reminding them that Title IX *requires* institutions of higher education to respond to claims of sexual violence on their campuses—and threatened institutions that didn't comply with the loss of federal funding. Subsequent letters followed that clarified expectations around handling cases of sexual violence and harassment, that required sexual assault education and prevention programming, and that mandated a new position of Title IX coordinator to handle all of the above, on campus. These new Title IX mandates sent schools scrambling to comply and many were wholly unprepared to uphold these expectations. At one point, more than three hundred colleges and universities were under investigation by the U.S. Department of Education for mishandling cases of sexual violence on their campuses.

Then in 2013, young women on college campuses began trying to force administrators to take sexual violence seriously. This movement was led by Andrea Pino and Annie E. Clark, two former college students featured in a documentary about sexual assault on campus called *The Hunting Ground*. Sexual assault scandals started breaking out all over the country, with ongoing national news coverage—so much so that the U.S.

Congress took up the problem of sexual violence on college campuses and what could be done about it. (I think that the courage of these college women and the national attention and press they received helped pave the way for #MeToo to catch fire in 2017.)

Since the end of the Obama administration in 2016, the Trump administration has rolled back many of these changes and expectations—to the deep upset of Title IX and victims' advocates everywhere. But the changes schools were forced to put into effect prior to the Trump administration seem to be carrying forward—which is at least some good news for sexual violence prevention on campus, victims, and victim advocates.

Emma Sulkowicz: "Carry That Weight"

Recent college graduate Emma Sulkowicz has also played a big part in empowering young women to find the courage to come forward about their experiences of assault. Emma spoke out against how her university handled (or perhaps better said, mis-handled) her own claims of sexual assault. Maybe you've heard about her already, read her story or seen her on the news.

Emma was a student at Columbia University in New York City. After she brought accusations of sexual assault against another student, the university found she did not adequately prove her case, and the young man was allowed to continue his studies on campus.

During the academic year 2014–2015, in protest of Columbia's response to her claim, Emma Sulkowicz turned her senior thesis into performance art. She carried her mattress everywhere—all over campus, to the library, to her classes—as a symbol and reminder of the sexual violence she endured while at Columbia, and to force everyone around her to *see* what normally goes unseen and unspoken.

By carrying her mattress—the mattress being a site of sexual violence—evidence of what happened to Emma was no longer private. She brought her mattress with her as a visible symbol of the enduring trauma she would have to carry inside her for the rest of her life. Other people were allowed to offer to help Emma carry her mattress, but her rule was that they had to *offer*—she couldn't ask for help.

Emma Sulkowicz's decision to do this made national news. She was suddenly everywhere, appearing on *Today*, a morning news show, and other news programs, raising awareness about sexual violence across the nation. Emma's statement and commitment to carrying her mattress for an entire academic year was lauded as heroic and drew peers and inspired strangers to offer to help Emma carry her mattress.

But Emma's senior thesis project was also controversial. Columbia University was not happy about Emma's project. She turned the spotlight of scandal on Columbia for the entire year she carried her mattress, all the way up to commencement. At the ceremony, Emma walked onstage to get her diploma and—after receiving it—finally set down her mattress once and for all, as parents, friends, and the press looked on. The alleged perpetrator had his defenders as well, who denied the assault and claimed that Emma's very public, year-long performance art had a lasting effect on his ability to continue his studies and on his reputation overall.

But the meaning of Emma's courageous effort was not lost amid all the attention. Emma Sulkowicz brought what is typically a very private, unseen trauma in the lives of women into the public space. She forced people to confront its reality and helped Title IX advocates to turn sexual violence on campus into a national topic of conversation.

Building a Culture of Consent

After reading so much about sexual violence and harassment, what it is and how victims are silenced and blamed, and what #MeToo has revealed about our world, you might be wondering:

How can we *stop* this?

How can we *change* this world so that sexual violence and harassment aren't such a common experience among so many people?

What can we do so that sexual intimacy and all that goes with it are truly a positive experience for all of us? For me, for you, for all the people we know?

I hope you are wondering these things.

They are some of the Biggest of Big Questions.

I've spoken to you already about culture, in particular, the problems and challenges I see in a *culture* of hooking up, and how they relate to these very issues. But I also think that some of the answers to these questions lie in forging a new kind of culture—one that springs from those ethical frameworks we've been building: a culture of *consent*.

Let's Stop and Think a Moment:

Have you ever had a conversation about sexual violence?

What about sexual violence prevention?

Spend some time writing down everything you've ever learned and been told about sexual violence—and how to prevent it. Afterward, I want you to spend some time evaluating these things. Do any of them sound like victim-blaming?

What Is Consent?

Consent Is About You and Who You Are

Here it is: the Biggest of Big Questions.

This is the moment when we delve into the complicated waters we've been heading into all along. This is the place where you stake out who you are, what you believe in, and how you value others. This is where your relational ethic comes to mean something even more than it does already, when you show yourself to be a person who is truly sexually empowered and liberated—someone who understands the meaning and value of sex, and the meaning and value of your partners. Where you show you are a person who is caring and just.

All of the above gets at this question:

What is consent?

Consent is the culmination of living out that relational ethic you began when you were a small child and formed your first friendships; when you started to learn all the things that friendship requires of you and does not require of you.

I'm not exaggerating or being melodramatic.

If there is anything I believe, it is this:

Consent—as a value, as a priority—gets right to the heart of who you are as a person, and who you are not. Whether you are a person who understands what it means to respect another person's humanity and another person's body, whether you respect your own self and your own body, and whether you believe in the dignity of all persons, including yourself. Prioritizing consent, valuing it, respecting its importance, is an expression of your humanity and the humanity of others.

And I want you to become utterly human on this front.

A New Lens for Sexual Liberation with Consent as Its Priority

If you've read this book all the way through, if you've spent time thinking about all the Big Questions I've offered here, if you've spent time considering some of the questions at the end of each of the chapters and the critical thinking that goes along with them, my hope (or my suspicion) is that you don't even need to do any further reflecting on consent. You don't need to because it's obvious you already know how and why consent is an essential requirement of any sexual activity. (Remember how I said that consent should be like a built-in? Or baked right in like chocolate chips into a cookie?) To not care about consent would be to violate your relational and sexual ethics in the most egregious way. You shouldn't need this lesson—none of us should need it.

But here we are because it's good to think directly about it, not just indirectly. It's important for us to take up the task of this Big Question and not just assume the answer is obvious.

This book, everything that comes before this chapter, is very personal to me. Because I've spent the last fifteen years of my life (perhaps more years, even, than you've been alive!) talking to students about sex and consent, I've also spent all this time pondering what, in the world, we could do better to empower those young women and men around sex and sexuality, and how in the world our sex education might be transformed so that consent becomes an obvious priority to every single one of us, and a given for any person who claims sexual empowerment.

I believe that true sexual liberation comes from a journey we take requiring us to answer the questions in this book with vulnerability and honesty, requiring us to build our own lens about sex and sexuality—what it means to us, what we want from our partners, and how we want to be as partners. I believe we must build it against and via all the many, sometimes empowering, sometimes destructive, nearly always conflicting stories and ideas and teachings we inherit from the world around us on this topic. I believe that true sexual liberation requires us to *not* simply take in those stories, ideas, and teachings uncritically, but in a way that makes us learn to become *critical* of these narratives. We must become empowered enough to judge whether or not the stories we inherit about sex, sexuality, and our partners are life-giving or soul-destroying to us and to the people around us.

Only once we learn to do such things are we on our way to becoming sexually self-possessed humans, on the cusp of also becoming empowered, respectful, ethical people in relation to sex and consent.

Only then are we on our way to building that sexually liberated utopia.

When it comes to *your* sexual ethic, my hope is that consent lies at its heart and that it becomes instinctual for you—just as good friendship can become instinctual for you once you've identified what is involved in relational ethics. The point of this book is to help you wade into the complexity of this subject, but also to get you comfortable accepting that complexity, learning to sit with it, becoming willing to embrace it. The more you are able to live with this tension and ambiguity, the more empowered and capable you will be to take on the responsibility that sexual intimacy requires of us in relation to our partners.

Is Consent a Yes/No Question?

The short answer is . . . no.

Consent is not simply *Yes, I want to do this* or *No, I don't want to do that.*

You can *reduce* it to this.

But I don't think it's good practice to reduce or oversimplify things. The Big Questions are here to help you become an examiner of life, a person with self-knowledge, an empowered, justice-oriented human—not simply someone who takes the easy route.

Consent is not about technicalities, such as the words you utter or don't, the words your partner utters or doesn't. You may have been taught that consent is just this—this very technical version of consent that involves speaking *yes* or speaking *no* out loud. But to equate *consent* with *yes* and *no* is to misunderstand the question and to misunderstand what consent is really about.

Maybe you disagree. Maybe you've seen "Tea Consent" on YouTube, and you've decided it *is* super simple and I'm making it way too complicated. But hear me out.

Whether or not your partner utters *yes* or *no* tells you nothing about whether or not the sex you are having is a performance (for example) for the sake of inherited rules and expectations that neither one of you agrees with or feels good about.

Saying *yes* or *no* doesn't deal with the presence of alcohol and how that might influence whether or how a person says *yes* or *no*.

Saying *yes* or *no* tells you nothing about how your partner understands the encounter, what they want from it, whether they want something more from it than just momentary sex, or whether or not they respect you and your body.

Saying *yes* or *no* does not convey a person's agreement to be objectified like a plastic sex toy (unless they specifically utter that out loud to you: "Treat me like a plastic sex toy, yeah, baby!").

Saying *yes* or *no* doesn't convey what they think of those stories that likely you both have inherited from culture, society, and your school community, and it certainly doesn't cover biases about gender, sexuality, race, and many, many other things.

Consent is not just about saying *yes* and *no* because every partner you have is different, and every sexual partnership you engage in is different. How you communicate with each partner will change, depending on your desires with them and their desires with you. Sexual partnership, ideally, can accommodate a range of desires and modes of communication, of what partners want to do, would like to try, and vice versa. Ideally, consent should be a celebration of many types of communication—the kind of intimate communication that is done with words, yes, but also bodies and gestures and glances and facial expressions.

Consent requires us to learn about our partners, to do many kinds of listening, seeing, and understanding. Good sex also requires this of us—which is why I believe that consent and good sex are reciprocal. Sexual intimacy has its very own language, and if we want to get good at it, we need to learn far more than *yes* and *no* as signals to our partners. It's like speaking Italian or French—quite beautiful when you are fluent.

Consent is also not just about saying *yes* and *no* because consent requires our *attention*. It involves us learning to pay attention to our partners, to look and see what they are telling us, to be willing to learn that language of gesture and body. Attention requires our patience, our willingness to observe, reflect, and think.

Consent is about desire, it's about living out who you really are and who you want to be in the context of sexual intimacy with a partner you respect and who respects you back. Consent is the antithesis of performance and pretense—it's supposed to help you become and show who you really are. It's supposed to draw out and encourage the expression of your true voice and your deepest desires and those of your partners, too.

And consent should be about far more than gaining a *yes* just because we want to avoid getting in trouble at school or even avoid criminal prosecution for assault. If your interest in someone's consent amounts to avoidance of future prosecution, then who are you, really? What in the world does that say about your humanity or lack thereof? What does it say about who you are as a person, a partner, a friend? (And why is our culture teaching consent as something that can be understood as a means to avoiding trouble, as opposed to something that expresses who we are as people?)

Consent *must* be about more than this.

It *must* express more than this.

When our society, our culture, our schools, and our workplaces present consent as though it is as simple as *yes* and *no,* we impoverish our sexual selves and the sexual intimacies we experience with our partners. Consent should express your understanding of sex and your respect for your partner. It should express your concern for their well-being, regardless of whether or not you want to pursue a future relationship with this person. If it doesn't do this, if you can't say to yourself, *I respect this person and care for their well-being for at least the course of the time in which we are sexually intimate with one another—*then you shouldn't be sexually intimate with them. That part *is* pretty simple.

Other Things Consent Is Not

If someone cannot speak words out loud because they are unconscious, if someone is too drunk to stand or passed out on a couch, they cannot consent.

You are probably saying to yourself right now, "Well, obviously."

Obviously a person cannot consent if they cannot communicate or if they are comatose. *Obviously* if someone is drunk to the point of passing out they cannot consent. Also, *why in the world* would you want to have sex with someone who can't even lift their head up or move?

Well, I am here, saying these things because it too often happens that people are sexually assaulted while they are incapacitated. Somehow we live in a world where a passed-out young woman on a couch is viewed as an opportunity for sex by someone or a group of someones. A world where humiliating and violating people who are incapacitated is seen by some as a good time and an opportunity to show one's manliness. We are here, saying these things because it is far too common that women in particular are victimized this way.

And though *I* know that *you* already know this, it still needs to be said:

By definition, sex, under these circumstances, is rape. It's assault. It's criminal.

We need to change the culture that perpetuates and enables such violence to occur and *you* need to be a part of that change. It is *all our responsibilities* to never become perpetrators of such violence, and in particular, such violence as an expression of masculinity. It is on *all of us* to disconnect this relationship between dominance and power with what it means to be a "real man." It is up *all of us* to separate, once and for all, entitlement to sex from being a powerful, popular, successful person. And it's on *all* of us to stop objectifying our partners. To stop idealizing the kind of sex that turns our partners into a means to an end, that turns their bodies into sites on which we *take* our pleasure, on which we *enact* our desires, as though these people *are actually non-human objects* we are meant to use and discard when we are done.

Most people understand the notion that to have sex with a passed-out person is, by definition, sexual assault. But it is that script, that story about using and objectifying and shrugging at one's partner that contributes to and perpetuates this idea that it is okay to have sex with a passed-out person. They live on the same continuum. And it is here that being "casual" about sex presents us a real paradox for consent.

We Cannot Have It Both Ways—So Let's Not Pretend We Can

I know: We always want it both ways.

We want to live the story we inherit about casual sex, that fairy tale of sexual liberation for all, *and* we want to prioritize consent when we are getting (casually) sexually intimate with people.

But I need you to recognize the conflict inherent in this desire.

Let's start by looking at the word *casual*.

To be casual is to be "unconcerned." To be able to shrug, to not care all that much, to be, perhaps, "whatever." The dictionary tells us that something casual is also "irregular," as in, it only occurs sometimes, once in a while, here and there. This, to me, sounds a lot like the values (or anti-values) of hookup culture—values that are problematic when we begin to think about consent.

Consent *is* a value—it involves showing concern for another's well-being. It is about caring for their well-being, listening to and respecting their desires. It is an ethical position in relation to another person. To prioritize consent is the opposite of being unconcerned.

Consent is casual's nemesis.

Then again, casual's synonyms are far more positive and sound like a recipe for a fun night of sex (so maybe this is where we got the idea of "casual sex" in the first place!). The word *casual* is synonymous with free, easy, uninhibited, open, informal, laid-back. Also, friendly, natural, relaxed. The list of awesomeness just continues.

Laid-back sex? That sounds great. Uninhibited, friendly, natural, relaxed, unceremonious, unpretentious, easygoing sex? That sounds fabulous. I love where casual is going right now. These synonyms sound perfect for a wonderful time with a partner—especially the *uninhibited, friendly, relaxed* ones.

However . . . But . . .

(I know. There really is always a but.)

Though casual sex, in theory, could be all these positive things—friendly, open, uninhibited—in practice and via a culture of hooking up, it has become none of these positive things, or it rarely does. Rather, it has absorbed the most negative possible interpretation of casual and codified that particular meaning into a norm that has been passed on and on (and will likely be passed on to you, too, if it hasn't already). By *codified* I mean "made rigid, scripted, *enforced.*"

While I am all in favor of uninhibited, natural, relaxed, unceremonious, unpretentious, easygoing sex, I am *not* in favor of *unconcerned* sex. *Unconcerned* is the opposite of *concerned*, and consensual sex is concerned sex. And you have to reckon with this. You have to *recognize* this.

You are welcome to have casual sex in the positive sense, because I think that kind of casual sex *could* also be consensual sex. But you will likely be passed on that other version of it, the kind that conflicts with consent. I don't want you to pretend that it doesn't conflict. I want you to be honest about what this version asks of people. I want you to open your eyes to it, pay attention to it, reckon with it.

Maybe it will be *your* generation that fixes how broken our notions of "casual sex" have become, reclaiming casual, sexual intimacy so that it becomes, *in reality*, that liberating, free, and easygoing kind of sexual intimacy that it was meant to be in the first place. The kind of casual sex that *is* compatible with consent.

But until that day? No more pretending.

No more pretending that the whatever, shrug-worthy, I-don't-care-about-you attitude people are trying so hard to bring to sexual intimacy is also compatible with the concerned, caring attitude that consensual sex requires. Don't buy that lie. Don't sell it either.

All Bodies Matter

There is no exception to this rule.

Every body is worthy of respect, of dignity, of pleasure, of tenderness. Every body is a site of vulnerability. Every body is an expression of our humanity.

Your body. Your partners' bodies. Regardless of gender, sexual orientation, race, ethnicity, disability, economic status, educational background, and every other particularity you can think of. Regardless of that person's reputation. Regardless of their popularity (or lack thereof).

No body is an object.

No body is the equivalent of a plastic sex toy.

No body. Never ever.

No body is entitled to another's body. It doesn't matter how god-like you are as an athlete, how rich your family is, how respected on campus you are, how popular, how powerful. No body has the right to abuse, disrespect, humiliate, enact violence upon another person's body. No body has the right to touch another's body against that person's will.

No body. Never ever.

It doesn't matter if culture and society and pornography and maybe even your school and then your college and then your workplace try and teach you a different story or tell you otherwise. Bodies are not to be used, abused, and discarded. No one has "the right" to do something to another's body because they happen to be more powerful, more popular, more privileged, more sober.

At the heart of consent is mutuality and reciprocity—mutual regard, mutual respect, a mutual understanding about the vulnerability of everyone's bodies, and a mutual agreement to listen to each other's bodies and the voices that come from those bodies about desire and lack thereof.

I hope that what I am saying is utterly obvious to you. It should go right along with the relational and sexual ethic you have been building all along.

The Good and the Bad of Sex, Committed, Consensual, and Otherwise: A Q&A

Does having consensual sex, does respecting and living by all of the above, does becoming an empowered, sexually self-possessed person mean that all sex will always be good, as in pleasurable and fun and thrilling?

Nope.

Sometimes the sex you have will be kind of crappy. There will be sex where there isn't pleasure or that isn't much fun or that is actually kind of boring and awkward or fumbling and just, well, kind of bad. Not-so-great sex is a part of life. Not-so-great sex is pretty much part of every long-term relationship. Sometimes you have amazing sex! And sometimes the sex is just, well, blah. But not-so-great-sex doesn't make it nonconsensual sex. Sometimes it just means it's not so great.

Sometimes after sex, you'll look back and say, well, I don't want to do that again because I didn't like it that much. Or you might conclude we just weren't very compatible. Or you might think to yourself, if I had known the sex was going to be so mediocre I would not have agreed to it. Blah. Oh well. Sometimes all the communication in the world between partners still doesn't fix sex in the pleasure and enjoyment and fun department. You try sex with someone, and it doesn't work out the way you hoped it would.

Sometimes after not-so-great sex, you might decide to try that again tomorrow and see if it can be better. And eventually it gets great as your partner and you figure out what you like and don't and how your bodies work and how to fulfill and listen to each other's desires. Sometimes it takes a lot of time and effort to figure out how to get to the good of sex for both of you and that journey itself is worth it.

Is consensual sex always sober sex?
Nope.

You can be drunk and have consensual sex. People do it all the time. People get tipsy, they get drunk, and they have really fun, very consensual sex. Maybe your parents even conceived you on some tipsy evening after dinner! (I know— you probably don't want to think about that.)

Let me back up. It's important that we are talking about consent in relation to alcohol, and the ways that alcohol can alter our ability to be aware of our own actions, and can mar our ability for conscious decision-making.

But I also worry that we are becoming overly literal about alcohol, sex, and consent, conveying that alcohol *always* affects consent and a person's ability to consent—which is simply not true. We are becoming literal about alcohol, sex, and consent because we are so afraid of complexity. We want easy answers to everything, obvious answers—but sex and consent don't work like that. You already know that consent is not just about *yes* and *no* because it's far more complex than these two words. Well, consent in relation to alcohol is complex, too.

You can have great drunken sex. You can also be sexually assaulted while drunk, or you can sexually assault someone else. You can be totally capable of consent while drinking. You can also lose your ability to consent because of drinking. But the alcohol isn't responsible for sexual violence. Alcohol doesn't *cause* sexual assault. *People* are the cause of sexual assault; perpetrators are the cause of sexual assault. This is a big, important difference, and I need you to understand this difference.

So you've started to get sexually intimate with someone—does that mean that the answer is yes, yes, yes *from there on out?*
No. Not at all.

Just because someone has decided they want to kiss you

once doesn't mean they want to keep kissing you, or that they want you to touch them, or because you've performed oral sex on them or they have on you that they want to have vaginal or anal intercourse with you (as an example). A person's consent can be withdrawn at any moment, any time, and you have to be prepared for this—and sensitive to and respectful of this communication.

If you are a guy, does that mean that you can't be the victim of a sexual assault?
No. Guys can be victims, too.

Anyone can be a victim, sadly. Victimhood doesn't discriminate based on gender identity. A cis guy can be a victim, a trans guy can be a victim, and a nonbinary person can be a victim—and in fact, trans and nonbinary folks are particularly vulnerable to sexual assault, regardless of how they identify.

Our biases about masculinity and what it means to be a "real man" can make it difficult, even nearly impossible, for guys to find the courage to come forward when they've been assaulted because they may worry, in doing so, that their identities as "real guys" will be shattered. That claiming themselves a victim will jeopardize their identities as men. But this doesn't mean that guys don't suffer from assault. As with women who are afraid to come forward because of the potential fallout, most guys who are victims suffer in silence, alone.

Is sexual assault only a heterosexual problem?
No. If only our sexual identities could act like shields against sexual violence—but they do not. Just as a victim can be of any gender identity, a victim can be of any sexual identity, too. Sadly, this also means that perpetrators can be of any gender or sexual identity. Sexual identity doesn't change the need for consent during sex. All sex requires it, and without it, someone, regardless of their particular identities, becomes a victim.

Is sex within a committed relationship always consensual?
A big *no* to this one, too.

People within committed relationships, people who declare love for each other, also commit sexual violence against each other. Sexual violence can happen between hookup partners who've just met. But you can also be married for twenty-five years to someone and end up sexually assaulting your spouse.

Commitment, relationship, love, even marriage—none of these are a 100 percent fail-safe against sexual violence. So much sexual violence occurs *within committed relationships*. Relationships and commitments do not always ward off violence. It is rare that sexual violence is committed by strangers—the rapist who jumps out of the bushes and holds a knife to your throat. A perpetrator is most likely someone we know, and may even be someone who has slept next to us for years.

This is the thing about sex, whether good or bad, with

someone you love or someone you've just met: It's a complex thing; it requires a developed-enough level of self-awareness and communication skills that empower us to live with the nuances and the tensions of this very human experience so we can learn to parse out what is consensual sex (and what is not).

Sexual Violence Prevention Is Everyone's Job

Regardless of gender or sexual orientation, it is *all our jobs* to prevent sexual violence. And not by *not* walking home late at night through the park, or by *not* going to the party at the "rape frat." That is not the prevention I'm talking about here.

It's everyone's job not to become a perpetrator of sexual violence.

It's everyone's job not to allow a "rape frat" to exist in our communities.

It's on all of us to *not* see and *not* allow others to see the body of a passed-out person as an opportunity for sex and for displaying our toxic masculinity to our guy friends. (And if we *do* see this happening to someone at a party, it's on all of us to call for help and do everything we can to stop this situation.) It's on all of us to interrupt and change the messed-up stories and "have-tos" and "shoulds" passed on to the next generation about sex and the meaninglessness of it and our partners.

For us to truly change the cultural attitudes toward sex that enable and perpetuate sexual violence, every single one of us must begin to take responsibility for the ways in which we have inherited and absorbed stories and ideas and expectations around sex that perpetuate and enable sexual violence. We have to become critical thinkers about ourselves, about sexual ethics, about sex (in general). I really believe that if we open up our culture, our society, our faith traditions, and our communities to the Big Questions about sex and consent, we will begin to transform our world from a place that enables and perpetuates sexual violence and puts the burden on victims to prevent it into a culture where sexual violence is rare.

This might sound utopian again and it might sound idealistic to argue that becoming thinkers about sex and consent, becoming truly empowered enough to ask these Big Questions, could change society in this way. But it's what I really believe. And what I hope with all my heart is that this might someday be true for you and for everyone you know. For all of us.

I want to live in a sexually liberated utopia. I really do.

Don't you?

Ethical Endeavors for Consent:

After reading this chapter, and the rest of this book, I want you to spend some more time with your relational and sexual ethics—I want you to sit down with them, study them, and ask yourself how consent fits into what you've already decided your ethic is.

Where is consent *implicit* in your relational and sexual ethics?

Now I want you to think about what you've read about sexual violence and consent in this last section, and ask yourself:
Is there anything missing from my relational and sexual ethics?

Expand your sexual ethic to include your answers to these questions, so that prioritizing consent is *baked right in*.

What Is Desire?

Tuning In to Our Deepest Desires

I want you to get what you want.

(Well, as long as it doesn't involve anything nonconsensual, criminal, or violent.)

Maybe you want to be loved more than you've ever been loved before and by someone you *like*-like, by someone who *wants you*–wants you. Maybe you are a girl and want to have roses delivered at school in front of everyone and maybe you are a *guy* and you want to have roses delivered at school in front of everyone and maybe you are nonbinary and you want the very same! Maybe you want to make out with someone for hours and hours on the beach. Maybe you want someone to write you a poem and post it on your locker door. Maybe you wish to go on a date, maybe you wish to ask someone on a date, maybe you wish that you didn't ever have to go on a date. Maybe you feel ashamed of wishing and yearning and desiring all these things plus the many other things that you are too embarrassed to mention.

Maybe you are ashamed of the kinds of things that turn you on. Maybe you think that no one else will be turned on by those things or that people will think you're weird for liking what you do. Maybe you are ashamed of who you seem to be attracted to. Maybe you are embarrassed about being a sexual person in general. Maybe you wish you didn't have any attraction to anybody at all. Maybe you *aren't* attracted to anybody and you feel ashamed about that.

I don't want you to feel shame about what you desire.

I don't want you to feel shame about *not* desiring something that someone else thinks you *should* want (but you just don't).

Shame gets in the way of our hearts and minds and souls and bodies and sucks the enjoyment out of life and love and sex. If you feel shame about your desires—be they not criminal or violent—I want you to climb over that shame like it's a wall in an obstacle course and leave it behind you.

Through desire, by learning to listen to our desires, to articulate them, we discover who we really are. Our desires *show* us so much about who we are. Listening to your own desires, learning to tune in to them like they are an old-fashioned radio station, is part of the journey you set out on at the beginning of this book.

It doesn't matter if what you might want happens to be a romantic cliché. Or that it might be *outside* of any of those clichés. What matters is that you:

* Try to understand where your desires come from. What scripts in our culture have planted these desires in you?

* Express your desires out loud and without shame.

* Ideally, fulfill those desires by living them in real life.

Wanting flowers (to take one example) is harmless—flowers are nice, a sweet gesture, and even if that flower-desire comes from scripts about what is romantic and what women are supposed to want from men (or what men are *not* supposed to want from anyone), who cares? If you like and want flowers, I'd like you to be able to enjoy receiving them as a gift from someone you have a crush on. What I *don't* want is for you to be embarrassed for wanting them. That doesn't do anything for you.

I want you to learn to listen to yourselves, your bodies, your hearts and minds and souls, dig deep in there and discover what you really long for underneath all the inherited noise of "I'm supposed to do this" and "We're all supposed to feel this or that and do this or that or want this and not want that." Often that noise, those narratives and scripts we inherit from all around us—our peers, social media (and pornography—more on that in a minute), our culture, our faith traditions, even sometimes our parents—can get in the way of figuring out what we *truly desire* deep down. I want you to find a way through all that stuff to *discover what you really, really want.*

Consider this another invitation.

I want you to think about desire. All kinds of desire!

Sexual, romantic, connective, emotional, relational, hot, bothered, etc., etc.

The sky is the limit! Go crazy!

Dig and dig and dig through all the muck of what other people have told you you're *supposed to* want or desire or yearn for so you can begin to dig up something real in there, something *yours*, something true to you. Something that makes your heart glow and expand and that makes your eyes light up and that three-letter word that's so hard to speak out loud sometimes: yes!

Starring in Someone Else's Story Versus Writing Your Own

In my interviews with college students, I asked every one of them a gazillion things about sex and hookups, and I asked every one of them this question, too: What about dating? Do people date here (at your college)?

The universal answer—no matter where I was or who I was speaking to—was *no*. "Nobody dates in college anymore." "Dating is something people did when my parents went to college but not here, not now, not me."

This first part of their answer conveyed the *inherited* narrative, but this inherited narrative was always followed by a *but*. "Nobody dates here, nobody wants to go out on dates," followed by, "*but* I wish they would." The cultural expectation was usually in conflict with the person's true desire.

Entire swaths of the college population were dealing with this conflict:

* Believing something that wasn't actually true about their peers (that nobody wanted to date, in this case).

* Which meant that no one was getting what they wanted (which in this case was the opportunity to go out on a date).

* Desires went unfulfilled.

Inherited narratives get in the way of people articulating their true desires out loud. College students are struggling with the reality that, even though *they didn't write* this story, *they are still expected to star in it.* They are expected to perform something that isn't true to them, and in the process of performing it, *they do not get what they want.* Their true desires are thwarted.

The college students I interviewed had similar experiences when I asked them what they thought about romance in an online survey.

The students were amazingly elaborate in their ideas about romance. Descriptions of romantic *settings* went on and on. Stuff like there'd be hundreds of candles lit in the room. Or hundreds of candles lit onstage in a darkened theater! There were also romantic picnics all over the place. On riversides and beaches and on the university's football field at night under the stars.

Nearly everybody mentioned two main elements essential to romance:

Romance involved *time*. Lavish amounts of time with someone who interests you romantically. And romance involved *talking*. Hours and hours to do this talking within the romantic
setting people dreamed up.

Romance = Connection.

Knowing and Being Known.

Romance, for most everyone, was about someone taking the
time to really figure out who *you* are, about giving you *space* to
be you, and in return, taking that time to give someone else all
these things, too. Romance was about showing a person they
were worthy of your time and your investment, of listening to,
getting to know, caring about, and getting attached to. The students' descriptions of romance were about everything they
weren't supposed to do or have in a hookup. Romance sounded
like a hookup's opposite.

But once again, students explained that, despite their *desire*
for romance, it wasn't something college students were "supposed to" want. The *but* in their answers was followed by the
inherited story. *Romance in college is dead. Once you're in college you're
not supposed to care about this stuff. We don't get be romantic in college.*

People felt embarrassed and ashamed about their wishes for
romance, too.

The dominant stories that students inherited thwarted *both*
their desires to date and to experience romance (that is, connection). These dominant inherited narratives narrowed their
choices, silenced their voices, and once again put them in a position to *perform* a role in someone else's story.

That's not liberation. That's not empowerment.

I don't want this struggle for you.

When it comes to desire, I want you to write your *own* story and star in it.

Why Is It So Difficult to Own Our Own Sexual Agency?

You know what I hear from people all the time?

Hookups *happen* in college. And sometimes hookups *happen* to you.

Or sometimes I hear this version instead:

Sex *happens* and sometimes sex *happens* to you.

There are so many problems with these statements.

First, there is the *consent* issue. Let's parse this out: sometimes hookups and/or sex "happens" to you. Happens, as in, you are standing there or lying there, as the case may be, and someone does something to you, and you passively receive it. As in, you don't actively *choose it*, you just *allow it* to be done to you.

I'm not saying that, by definition, this is sexual violence. But I *am* saying that consent in these circumstances is murky. That it's not easy to pinpoint a person's consent here.

People who describe sex and hookups this way are pushing off their own sexual agency. They are not saying, "I *wanted this* so I *went after it*". Or "yes, yes, *yes*, I loved that hookup and wanted that hookup to happen!" They are showing ambivalence, giving that shoulder shrug, that *whatever* about sex and hookups and saying that "sex happens" as though it's something floating in the air, and you catch it like you might catch a cold.

They aren't *affirming* their own sexual agency.

They aren't *claiming* it.

I would rather hear, "I wanted to hook up, I *chose* to hook up, and so *yeah,* I hooked up!!!! YEAH!!"

In addition to consent being murky, sexual desire is also missing from the equation. That *wanting* of another person, that *wanting* of their body that comes from all sorts of places in your body.

What I long to hear is a story that goes something like: So I was at a party, and across the room I saw this person and this person was *hot*. Like, I was *so attracted to them* that I just had to have them. So I went over to them, I met them, I flirted, they flirted back, and then we were like, *We have to have each other!* So we went off and made out and did whatever else for however many hours and it was *so hot* and pleasurable and fun and I wanted it so badly and so did they and it was fantastic.

This story sounds very different from, "Yeah, so sex probably will happen to you while you are in high school or college."

I want you to *own* the sexual activity you participate in.

I want you to *want* it.

I want you to *want* your partners.

I want you to *listen* to your body's desires.

I want you to *own* your sexual agency—period.

I want you to *claim* it—which involves *claiming enthusiastically* the sex you have and the partners you have it with, and which also involves you *getting comfortable* with your own desires and expressing those desires.

I *don't* want consent and sexual desire to be murky at best for you, or at worst, not there at all.

There are challenges to this kind of claiming. Challenges to owning one's sexual agency. These challenges involve facing a culture that tells you to shrug at sex and also at your partners (be "whatever" about them). It requires you to face the possibility that by owning your own sexual agency and your desires, you might be rejected sometimes. It involves reckoning with the gendered nature of sexual desire, too—as in, while men are supposed to be obsessed with having sex, regardless of sexual orientation, *women are not.* Sexual agency is more complicated if we identify as women, because women and girls who *enthusiastically* go after sex, who *claim* their sexual agency with gusto, risk being labeled sluts, which is super unfair, ridiculous, and the definition of sexist.

But . . .

You've got to wade into these waters. You've got to face this reality with eyes open, with bravery, with courage. I don't want you to be afraid of your own sexual agency. I don't want things like slut-shaming to get in the way of you doing this. I want you to want the sex you have. I want you to claim sex as yours and as fantastic and fun. I want you to take those risks of rejection because owning those risks means you are empowered and secure enough to take them.

I'm not saying it won't be difficult. But I am saying that it is super important and that I *want* this for you. I want it pretty bad.

Learning to Listen to Our Bodies

Remember how I said earlier on that my parents told me nothing about sex? Well, when I was your age, I didn't know anything. Like I said, I had to go searching in my mother's romance novels for advice. This was back before the internet existed (I know—I'm super old!) so it's not like I could easily look up sex. My friends didn't know anything either.

And, I'll tell you a secret:

I learned a lot about sex *by doing*. As in, if I felt like making out with someone—if this seemed like a good idea—and they felt like making out with me, then make out we did. And if we felt like going further, then we did! We just kind of went with it, and let our desires be our guide.

And I know: This sounds like a terrible idea for sex ed.

But...

This trial and error, this learn-by-doing/wanting method for sex, as bad as it sounds, actually taught me one of the best lessons when it comes to sex:

To listen to my body.

What does my body want? What do I want to do? What sounds like a good idea and a not-so-good idea? What sounds fun and not so fun? What is my body telling me *it* desires? What feels good and what doesn't? Do I like this? Yes! Okay, great! I'd like to do that again then! But that other thing you just did? I didn't like it so let's skip that next time, all right?

Because nobody really taught us anything (which I am not advocating as an ideal method for sex education), I didn't have many of those inherited voices crowding my brain with ideas about what was *supposed to* happen or what I was *supposed to* want or do or like or not like or expect or not expect. This turned out to be pretty liberating, by today's standards.

The narratives that get passed on to us often teach us *not* to listen to our bodies, our desires, to what we really want. They tell us what we're *supposed to* want and then make us feel ashamed if our real desires differ. They tell us this is what you're *supposed to* do, and if you don't do it then something is wrong with you. That you're weird.

An amazing psychologist, Deborah Tolman, made a really smart distinction with respect to how young adults today—girls especially—experience desire. Or rather *don't* experience it.

She talks about desire versus desirability.

Tolman argues that girls are raised to *become* and *act* desirable. Girls learn to wear sexy outfits, pose in a sexy way, put on a sexy face, even do sexy sexual things. But their idea of "sexy" doesn't come from within or from a relationship with a partner. It comes from pornography, from photos and culture and societal expectations and pop stars, and today from social media among other online sources. Girls aren't growing up to figure out what sexy means *to them*, what makes them *feel* sexy, what turns them on sexually, what they *actually desire*. Girls are learning to *perform desirability* for others, often without having any idea what they actually desire themselves.

I don't want *you* to grow up learning how to become desirable according to outside, inherited standards, especially the kind you learn from porn. I want you to learn to listen to your own body's desires, your brain's desires, your soul's desires, your heart's desires. Because I believe your body knows more about what it wants than you might think, or give it credit for.

Which brings us to porn. Yup. We're gonna go there. We gotta.

Yeah. So, Let's Talk About Porn

I'll be honest: I am not a fan of porn.

I think porn is super problematic.

In *theory*, porn is fine. I have nothing against people watching people have sex. Technically, there is nothing wrong with this.

However. (And this is a big however.)

Porn and the porn industry in *reality* is so messed up I could write an entire book about why it's so messed up. I want you to think very, very carefully and critically about porn in your own life—whether you decide to watch it and how it might affect you and the sex you have and the partners you have it with.

First, most porn is sexist to a level that can't be fully described in this tiny section. Most porn is about heterosexual men, or in theory, it caters to heterosexual men. It's not usually made with women and their desires in mind, or the desires of LGBTQ people. (There *is* porn that caters to women and LGBTQ people, but it is still pretty rare.) Porn sex is generally about men having sex, about men getting to fulfill (stereotypical, problematic) masculine desires, and about watching women perform those desires for men. Porn is not *real*, as in, the sex you watch is *not* realistic, especially in terms of how it reflects women and how women act. Often porn is about women doing things to men that women would not normally want to do to men if they were not acting in a porn flick. And very often, porn features violence against women.

Yes. Violence against women. As in, rape. Sexual assault.

So much of the porn industry is based on and thrives on violence against women and also children.

The other major problem with the porn industry is the fact that so much online porn is not legitimate. As in, it does not feature actors and actresses who are paid, but often trades off and preys upon people (usually women, young girls and boys, sometimes even toddlers) who are not there of their own volition. I am not saying that all porn is like this—plenty of porn is "legitimate." But you can't turn away from the fact that the world's appetite for online porn, more and more illicit and violent porn, has not been good for the most vulnerable populations of women and children around the world.

Then there's *you* and porn.

You've probably already watched some. And you've probably done this out of curiosity. And curiosity is awesome. Sexual curiosity is totally normal and good. I applaud it. I support it. I encourage it. And I get it—we're curious about sex, so watching porn seems logical, because when we watch porn, we can see how sex is *done*. How it happens. What it looks like. Sort of.

But then, not really (because you have to remember that it's a performance—porn is acting, all of it, when it's not assault). So there's *that* part.

But the real lesson we learn about sex from porn?

When we watch porn sex, we can see how *porn sex* is done.

Porn sex is not usually a good representation of the sex that *you* will likely have or want to have, or the sex that your *partner* will want to have. It's usually not a good representation (and often an awful, distorted representation) of both women's and men's bodies. So what you learn from watching porn sex is how to have porn sex—and more likely, how to *perform* porn sex.

To sum up: Porn sex teaches us to *perform* porn sex.

What porn does *not* teach us is about listening to our bodies and our bodies' desires. Porn teaches people a very particular idea about what is *desirable* to do during sex, but it doesn't teach anyone anything about the authentic and actual experience of fulfilling one's desires during sex. Porn teaches desirability without desire. Which means that porn often alienates us from our own desires and discourages us from discovering our own desires. And what we are told is desirable during porn sex is usually pretty crazily warped, especially for women.

Which is why, again, I'm not a fan of porn.

I don't want you to put on a good performance during sex. I don't want you to impose porn ideas about sex onto girls and women, and if you identify as a girl or a woman I don't want those ideas to be imposed upon you. I want you to locate sexual desire much closer to home—right inside your body and the bodies of your partners. I want sexual desire to emerge from the relationship you have with your partner, and not to come from without, from some video you watched that is not personal to you at all, or to your partner either.*

Real sex is not only better than porn sex, the best part about it is that it is *real sex*.

———————

* One caveat about LGBTQ porn.

LGBTQ porn can be *really* important if you identify as LGBTQ— especially if you live within a community or circumstances that try to forbid your sexual identity from existing, and forbid LGBTQ sex altogether. Porn can be a lifeline for people who otherwise have no access to or education about sex for LGBTQ people. I'm not saying that LGBTQ porn is perfect or doesn't come with all the same problems I've mentioned above. But sometimes it offers the only access to understanding sex that a young person might have—and it can be *affirming* of one's sexual identity and of LGBTQ sex in general. And I want that for you—affirmation.

You still need to be smart about porn, though—critical about it, know the stereotypes you are witnessing when you watch it, the potential for violence and the ways that porn promotes the sexual slavery of women and children around the world.

Some Dilemmas of Desire:

Do you know what *you* desire?

I don't mean just with respect to sex or your body. I mean about all kinds of things in your life. Like, what about your activities? Do you do them because someone else told you you should, or because it will someday be good on a college application? Or do you do them because you *love* them, enjoy them, have fun while doing them? And what about school stuff? Do you have a favorite subject? Have you ever wondered what your favorite subject is? What about how you spend your free time? What things do you most look forward to doing? Who are your *favorite* people to spend time with? Do you love playing a sport or watching a particular sport? Or do you play a sport that you used to love but now you kind of dread it?

And speaking of dread . . .

What are the things in your life that you dread most? Things that you don't look forward to doing at all—that even make you feel bad about yourself, or that you have to force yourself to do? Things that *other* people have decided you should do for the sake of your future, but that you only do begrudgingly?

Sometimes we have to do things we don't love—like get our homework done even in subjects we really dislike because one day we need to graduate. But it's important, in the effort to gain self-knowledge, that you begin to understand what you *love* doing, what you *wish* you could do more, the kind of people in your life who, after spending time with them, you walk away feeling like the world is a good place to be and that you like being in it. I want you to learn to listen to those feelings—to follow them. As you get older, following your heart in this way is important toward the end of leading a happy, fulfilling life. And once you learn to do this in lots of areas of your life, then listening for those desires that come from your body, desires that have to do with who you are attracted to and sexual intimacy, will come naturally to you.

I want you to open your journal and make an inventory of desires, by answering the questions above about what you look forward to, and what you don't.

What Is Love?

So Many Kinds of Love!

I want to bring up something that so rarely enters the conversations we have about sex and consent: *love*. We may love *love*, but it confounds us, too. Intimidates us even as it intrigues us.

And the English language is funny about love.

Lots of languages have multiple words for love because there are so many different types of love. Loving a parent is different from loving a book is different from romantic love is different from loving playing a sport or loving baking.

In Spanish, you would use the verb *amar* for lasting, intense romantic love; *querer* for the love you feel for your siblings or your parents or even your cat; and *encantar* for the things you love in life, maybe your bedroom or your favorite music group or your favorite sweatshirt or how you feel when you are playing soccer or the piano. *Querer* and *encantar can* be interchangeable, but you definitely wouldn't use *amar* to describe what you feel for your sibling or that T-shirt you live in because you've had it forever and it's so comfortable.

In Greek, there are seven different words for love, including *eros,* which has to do with erotic, romantic love (like *amar*), and *philia,* which has to do with the kind of love shared between friends.

I could go on, listing the many distinctions between types of love in languages other than English.

But in English, love is love is love, even though when we take the time to think about it, we can distinguish between many kinds of love that most of us are lucky enough to experience in life. *You* can distinguish between the many kinds of love you feel. You already know that the love you feel for your parents and your sisters and brothers is different from your love for history or math, which is also different from the love you feel for your first romantic partner, which is different from your love for basketball.

Love is important—all kinds.

Love is complicated and also wonderful.

To love is a fundamental part of what it means to be a human.

Philosophers, novelists, poets, theologians, psychologists, and every kind of artist and thinker have devoted entire treatises and books and plays and paintings to reflecting on love, to celebrating love, exploring love, yearning for love, missing love, trying to decide what in the world love is and where it comes from and why we feel it. Shakespeare loved love, Plato loved love,

Jane Austen loved love, and they are in good company with a gazillion other people who have waxed poetic (literally) about love in their work.

But, for some reason, we are now teaching people to separate love from sex—at least until they plan to get married. And I want us to think on that for a bit.

Yearning for Love

I've noticed a pretty weird trend over the years.

It's a trend that unfortunately coincides with those expectations to perform something that isn't authentic to you, and all this "I'm not allowed to, I'm not supposed to, I can't because by now I need to be over wanting to do that" business. The very stuff that I do *not* want you to struggle with. Because, well, it's not very empowering and it's not very conducive to people getting to fulfill their desires, desires which sometimes include loving and being loved.

The trend is this: We are learning—and we are teaching kids, people like you—that falling in love will get in the way of fulfilling your professional and academic goals, especially when you go to college. We are somehow sending the message (whether intentionally or not), that falling in love is a problem, that it somehow will thwart all the things you want to accomplish.

"We're not allowed to fall in love."

A group of my students once explained this to me (while practically weeping) after we read Patti Smith's heartwrenching, exquisitely beautiful memoir *Just Kids*, about her love affair with the photographer Robert Mapplethorpe. Their relationship started when they were just seventeen, and they were so madly in love that they moved in together in Brooklyn.

The theory about why you're not supposed to fall in love-while-young these days goes something like this: Because love can capture you fully, because it can be so all-consuming, and because committed, loving relationships take time and work and, well, *commitment*, and because you are so busy with your million activities and all your academics and fulfilling your extensive professional aspirations and trying to live up to the very high expectations of everyone around you, *you do not have time for love*. Love and being in love will turn your head from the prize, which is success in academics and a future dream job. You can love people later, when you are getting ready for marriage, which is, when? I don't know, maybe after you turn thirty?

To sum up the message:

Love and success do *not* go hand in hand.

Love ≠ Success in Life.

(Until marriage, that is.)

This message may get extra-emphasized if you identify as a woman—and for really important, very valid reasons. The theory *here* goes, that if you are a career-focused, academically centered and accomplished young woman, and if you allow yourself to fall in love while you are too young, all those dreams *especially for you* could automatically go *poof*. The reason? Because still, today, women bear the brunt of domestic responsibility. Because people fear that women will prioritize the love relationship over everything else and may even be asked by their partner (especially if the partner is a man) to prioritize *his* career and success over her own; and that a woman will agree to do so because of how girls and women are still raised to consider their own desires last after everyone else's. And also because sometimes with love there comes marriage very quickly, and even children very quickly, and having a child is pretty much still a career-killer for a lot of women. (Talking about why that is and how terrible that is and what we might be able to do to fix that reality would take another entire book to explain, so I'm leaving it there.)

I know. The world is not fair to women and girls in this regard. (Or in many other regards.)

But . . .

One of the main reasons people have learned to divorce sex from connection, from emotion, from attachment is the message that love will get in the way of your success. Simultaneous with this message about love is the message you likely get about sex—that it's normal to be having it during high school and college. "It's normal to have sex, but don't fall in love. Have lots of sex but beware love." Hookups are meant to provide you the sex without any feeling for your partner, protecting you from the danger of possibly having an interest in your partners. You can get your sex done but do so like robots! (Super, super fun-sounding, I know.)

I am not here to say that you have to be in love to have sex. I don't think you do, actually. I'm just saying that sometimes it's nice to love the person or people you have sex with, and it's totally okay if you'd like to love and be loved back. Your desires are your desires, and if this is one of them, I'd like you to be able to fulfill it at some point, whenever you are ready, and that might mean really soon or it might mean when you are sixty-five years old and about to retire.

Also. The idea that success and love can't go hand in hand is false—even if you identify as a girl or woman.

There is absolutely no reason you can't love someone and still pursue your dreams and fulfill your academic expectations and professional aspirations and all that stuff. And it's absolutely and totally okay if you discover (if you happen to fall in love) that love gives you some new and different priorities, other than the kind of academic, professional, and financial success everyone is saying you should care about more than anything else while you are a young adult.

Part of growing up, of working hard, of dreaming big, of experimenting with sex and love and romance and dating and relationships is discovering yourself. To discover who you really are and *what you really desire* in life. To figure out what makes you happy. To figure out what you love most in life—and I mean that in every sense of the word *love* in any language. What you love to do, who you love to be with, what you love to read, what you'd love as a career, whether you love history more than marketing and whether soccer is the sport for you or your true love is ballet. (Love and desire are super-close siblings by the way.)

I started this book by saying I want you to become a critical thinker about yourself, and this desire of mine extends to love.

Part of knowing yourself is letting yourself have experiences.

And I think that part of sexual experimentation involves risking our hearts to others, and experiencing all that goes with this, including heartbreak. Sometimes it also means choosing to love over everything else, like Patti Smith and Robert Mapplethorpe did (and their careers ended up being pretty amazing, so choosing love didn't end up hurting them). Love—just like the college you go to and the major(s) you choose and the activities you pursue—opens up new doors to you and opportunities and happinesses in life. It's okay (I promise) to let your heart be your guide sometimes, or even a lot of times. You'll discover so much about yourself if you do.

I *also* think it's important for you and your love partner to be self-aware about some of the good, well-intentioned reservations people might have about your falling in love and why that might cause you to forfeit your dreams (especially if you identify as a woman). But I also have faith that if you are becoming a critical thinker about all the Big Questions in this book, you are also going to be thinking about those possibilities and watching out for those potential pitfalls automatically.

And just as there isn't any one-size-fits-all approach to sex and sexuality, there isn't a one-size-fits-all timeline for love. Love happens, and often we can't do much about it other than embrace it and enjoy the ride as we do. Don't turn yourself away from it on purpose. Love is a gift. Experiment with it, just like you would anything else.

Love and Self-Knowledge

You already know so much about love, even if you've never been "in love" before, in a romantic sense.

Friendship involves love. Being in a family involves love. You have pets that you love. You have people in your life that you love and who love you back. There are aspects of the world that you love and will fight for. Maybe you love the ocean and worry that we are destroying it, and you feel compelled to work to preserve the beautiful beaches and sea where you've grown up or where you've vacationed with your family. Or maybe it's the forests or maybe it's the animals.

Love compels us to do things, sometimes for others, sometimes for nature. Sometimes that compulsion is a pleasure, sometimes it is an obligation, but we do it because love teaches us what is right to do and what is not, and when we must rise to the occasion. Love asks of us many things on behalf of someone or something else, and, ideally, love offers us the same in return. Love expands us, moves us into spaces we would not go otherwise. Love teaches us empathy. Love opens our hearts and minds and souls and teaches our bodies the value of being vulnerable to another person; it teaches that when we *are* vulnerable there exist people in the world who will treat us with tenderness, with respect, and with dignity. Love makes life more meaningful.

But you already know this.

What I want is for you is to learn how to *listen* to what your heart tells you about yourself, about others, about your interests and your life pursuits. It's become difficult to do this with all the many messages we receive about who we should be and how we should act, and what needs to get done for success in life, be that social success, academic success, or career and financial success. It's like we're all old-fashioned radios that can't remember how to tune in to what our hearts tell us.

Self-knowledge—becoming a critical thinker about yourself—is connected to your heart, which is connected to love, which is ultimately connected to living a good and happy life. There are so many things that I want for you, one of which is the freedom to love whenever you are lucky enough to find love in your path. Another is to have enough knowledge of yourself and your own desires to pursue a life and career and interests that fulfill you truly. The skills of self-knowledge and critical thinking help alert us to what is right for us to do and to pursue in life, and also *who* is right for us to invest ourselves in, and *when* it is right for us to make that investment. Self-knowledge and critical thinking help us learn how to love and what to love and when to love, too.

The beauty of falling in love with someone also involves how this experience transforms and reorders our life and priorities in ways that we can't control—and shouldn't always try. This is love's magic and also the thing about love that likely scares us. It is so powerful it draws us out in ways we don't expect and can't predict. Love is risky in this way, and in taking this risk, we grow and change and transform and become new selves and then new selves again.

Wow. Amazing. Truly.

BTW: Heartbreak Is Part of Life

"Love makes you weak."

This is another thing I've heard a lot. That because love makes us vulnerable to another person, because it makes us beholden to them, that this is a problem. The ways that love makes us want to be with someone all the time, the ways it makes us unable to stop thinking about that person, how love makes us need another person in ways we never before knew we could need someone, that these are problems. There is a message out there, floating around in the culture, that to allow yourself to be vulnerable in this way means that something is wrong with you. You have failed to be strong and *invulnerable*. We are taught as we grow up to associate love with "clinginess," to associate love with a loss of power, because the someone you love becomes a person who holds power over you.

This is such an impoverished idea about love.

It's one born of fear.

The fear lies in taking the risk of loving someone. Yet since when has fear of taking a risk made a person strong? It's quite the opposite, isn't it? We show strength *when we take the risk*. This is why there is strength in vulnerability, and why in vulnerability, there is such reward. In vulnerability, in risk-taking alongside another person, we stand to gain Meaning with a capital M. We stand to gain a glimpse into our life's purpose. We stand to gain the possibility of being loved.

But it is also and always true that allowing ourselves to love someone can end in pain and heartbreak. *You* know this as well.

Most of us have loved and lost in life, even while very young. Sometimes we lose a beloved pet. Some of us lose people, a grandparent, or in circumstances of great tragedy, a parent, a sibling, a friend from school. When we open our hearts to another, when we allow ourselves to love something or someone, we always risk the pain of losing them—whether because of death or because of circumstances like a move across the country, or because they tired of us or they simply stopped loving us even as we continued to love them.

That is why romantic love can be so scary. And friendship love, too.

All of us have lost a friend at some point, a friend who found someone else to invite over to their house instead of us, or who moved on to another friend group or social status without us, maybe even a best friend. Eventually, we all know the pain of losing a romantic partner, someone we fell in love with and who loved us back, at least for a time, but then the relationship ended.

The pain from this loss of love—be it romantic love or friendship love—can put us off loving in general. That grief can be pretty unbearable and all-consuming. It can make us never want to take that risk again, for fear of experiencing that tremendous pain again, of having to get used to our lives again without those people we loved in it. To learn to endure this heartbreak without hardening ourselves to loving again is one of life's most difficult lessons. It is part of what makes us human, our capacity to love and be hurt by the loss of that love.

But I don't want fear of pain to stop you from loving and being loved. You would miss out on some of the greatest moments and experiences of your life. I want this just as much as I don't want you to let messages that teach you that love will get in the way of success to stop you from loving and being loved. Love changes us in ways thrilling and painful and unexpected, love reorients us, love expands us, love scares us, and love makes us happy. Even with all the risk involved in loving, I want you to become fearless in the face of love and all that it can bring, both good and painful. I want you to learn to listen to the desires of your heart, so that when love comes your way, you can let yourself fall.

Then maybe someday people will read *your* memoir about the person you loved madly when you were young and wish that they, too, could have that much beauty in their lives. That they, too, could have as much courage as *you*.

I Want You to Have a Love Fest!

I want you to select three books/stories from the list in the back of this book and read them. After reading each one, I want you to write in your journal about what you think the story, the characters, the writer, is saying to you about love. And reflect on what you think of it.

After you read *all* three, I want you to spend some time with your relational and sexual ethic, asking yourself where love fits within them.

To help: Make a list of all the things you already know about love, from your own experience of loving the people, animals, and things all around you and in your life.

A Culture of Consent?

Let's Build a World, an Ethic, a You Where Sexual Violence Is No Longer

What would it be like to live in a world that is free of sexual violence? A world where all of us are raised to become the best, truest, and most honest versions of ourselves? Where *performing* inherited cultural norms that make us uneasy or that get in the way of fulfilling our desires was not something expected of us as we grow up?

What would it be like to live in a world that celebrates sexual diversity and all LGBTQ people? A world where boys and men can really be *real* and be the vulnerable, openhearted humans so many of them wish they could be? A world where girls and women are not diminished for simply being girls and women and where women's bodies are not automatically regarded as sites for violence? A world where we don't create

285

pyramids of power and patriarchy that seat white, heterosexual men at the top, and where the farther you get from that "ideal" identity because of gender, race, sexual orientation, or disability, the less power, the less respect, the less *value* you have according to patriarchal, heterosexist, racist culture and society?

What would it be like to live in a world where bodies are *never ever* disposable? No bodies, not one single body? Where all bodies are regarded as worthy, regardless of gender, sexual identity, race, economic privilege, education?

WOW, I'd like to live in that world.

Wouldn't you?

To me, it sounds like it might be that sexually liberated utopia I keep bringing up. A world where everyone, *you* included, is raised to become a sexually self-possessed, sexually self-aware, sexually empowered person. A world where you becoming all these things is a *goal*, even *the* goal, as opposed to something to fear or work against.

This world, the one I describe?

I know, with all my heart, that it would also promote what I've come to think of as a culture of consent.

What Is a Culture of Consent?

A culture of consent is the opposite of a culture of hooking up.

It's the opposite of a culture where systemic sexual violence and harassment are perpetuated and enabled, where that insidious stuff is baked right in.

A culture of consent is *not* a culture that expects everyone to be saying *yes* to sex all the time or that expects everybody to be obsessed with sex, having sex, constantly. Nope. That's not it.

Because a culture of consent is an *anti-performance* culture (unless you're actually, for real, on a stage because you're a theater person. Then it's totally pro-performance! Break a leg!).

But I also say these things because, in my work toward the goal of creating a culture of consent, one of the places I've received pushback is from religious communities and leaders who are concerned that fostering and prioritizing consent on a cultural level will somehow teach *all* people—including children and young adults within religious communities—that they *must* be having sex. I want to be very clear and up front that *no*, absolutely not. This is not what I have in mind when I speak of a culture of consent.

A culture of consent would accommodate a range of relationships, timelines, and viewpoints with respect to sex because, well, consent would be at its heart. And when consent becomes a priority, when it's the value that is at the center of a culture, this means that *respect for desire, need, ethics, and individuality* are inherent. A culture of consent is *not* a performance culture, it's not a culture that *pressures* someone to be a person they are not. It aims to empower all people to live out who they really are, the commitments and values important to them, in a culture that understands everyone is different, and that there is no one-size-fits-all approach to sexuality or timeline to love, either. If your approach is to abstain from sex, then this fits perfectly within a culture of consent, too.

But if your approach is to try to fit everybody into the same-sized sex attire, as religious traditions are wont to do, and if your approach is anti-LGBTQ? Well, yeah. A culture of consent would not support you on that front. Sorry, not sorry.

I've said a lot about what a culture of consent is *not*.

So what *is* it, then, anyway?

A culture of consent is one that prioritizes sexual and relational ethics—that's for sure. It prioritizes all that stuff I mentioned in the intro and in the sexual ethics chapter, stuff like human dignity and justice, all the values I've offered as foundational to your thinking about relationships and with your partners. Like vulnerability and caring and tuning in to all that desire swirling around inside of you.

A culture of consent encourages all the work you've been doing to figure out *your* ethics throughout this book. It supports this ongoing journey you've begun, to figure out who you are as a sexual being. It celebrates diversity of all kinds and equality for all humans. It's a culture that helps you learn who you really are, and grow up to be a person you are so proud to be! Confident in yourself, honest about your desires, open about your yearnings to love and be loved, respectful of all others, excited and curious about sex, and accompanied in the journey of your life by fulfilling relationships that cross generations.

It sounds pretty good, doesn't it?

I think so.

And I want it for you. I really do.

That's one of my deepest, most personal and profound desires in this life.

Learning to Take a Walk in the Center of Yourself

Cutting Through All the Noise

One last thing before I go.

I know you are super-busy and super-connected and super-on call.

Today we live as though all of us are heart surgeons.

I want to come back to that topic I started out with at the beginning of this book, about self-knowledge, and figuring out what makes you *you*. I want so many things for you—a healthy, empowered sex life; pride about your sexual identity and gender, whatever those turn out to be; respect and care for your partners and the same from them to you.

But I also want you to cultivate a space inside yourself that you can go to when you need it.

Maybe it brings you peace, maybe you call it your soul, or maybe it's simply a safe space. Where you can contemplate all the complexities of life, not just about sex but about any aspect of your humanity that longs for safety in that tension and confusion of questioning, of not having an easy answer.

I would like you to dedicate this time and space to yourself, for yourself.

I will be up front (like I always am!) and say that I believe it requires you to disconnect from your phone, to listen to what comes up in your mind and your body and your heart when you've freed yourself from the noise of constant connection. But it doesn't necessarily need to be a time and space where you are alone. Maybe you'll invite your most trusted companions in life to talk to you there. Or maybe it is you by yourself, in your bedroom, or in the woods, or under the water as you swim. I believe that in these spaces of withdrawal within ourselves and that we seek within the world, we not only find ourselves, but we also find out who we most want to be in the company of others. We discover who and what we love, and we discover the things that we love about ourselves.

And I want this for you—to discover many kinds of love for self and other.

Ages and ages ago, Henry David Thoreau went into the woods to live alone, to cut through the noise of the world, to live more slowly, more authentically. It's remarkable to me how much his description of the world's ills from the late nineteenth century describe the ills of our world right now. He longed to be awake to life, to slow down and enjoy the tiniest of delights and sounds and moments, to not sleepwalk through the world like a zombie.

I want you to be awake, too.

I don't want you to sleepwalk through your life, accepting the stories the world tells you about yourself without even knowing who you are, or caring to know you. The stories you are given about how you should be, stories that the world tells you to accept without question, as though every story should be one size fits all when of course they are not. I want you to write your own stories and then live them out on terms that you set, on terms that allow dignity and respect and choice and voice to flourish in your life and the lives of others. I think the more that we become the people we are meant to be, the more all the questions in this book become possible to navigate ethically and well.

Thoreau retreated from the noise of the world, quite literally, by going to the woods and living in a cabin. I don't believe that this is, literally, necessary. But the one last question I have for you is this:

What is your metaphorical cabin in the woods?

Your last Big Question is to answer *this* question. Where do you go to disconnect from the noise, the fast pace of the world, and the expectations around you, all the things pressing on you? I want you to decide what that place is, to commit to going to it regularly, so you have a space to contemplate all that our humanity and being a human person asks of us. And so you have this place inside you, a kind of refuge that reminds you who you really are or that helps you answer a particular question when you realize it needs revision. A safe place to keep your compass, so that when you are feeling lost, you can remember how to find your way through.

ADVICE TO OUR YOUNGER SELVES PART IV

"Your body is your own. When you're thinking about what you want to do, what you don't want to do, or what you're feeling, remember to put yourself first. Your culture, the images you see on television, the expectations of your friends, none of those get to define you. Only you do that. It's okay to say no to hug or a kiss on the cheek just because you don't want to. Just because a little voice inside you is telling you, I don't want this. Listen to that voice. That voice is you. Sometimes, maybe, that voice is going to say yes. That's cool, too. You may have a crush. You may not. You may change your mind. All those feelings are valid. No one should make you feel they're not. You were raised to respect others. Do that. But remember, respect is a two-way street. Your choices and your voice deserve respect, too. No one should ever pressure you or make you feel bad about your choices. You may be confused sometimes. You may have questions. That's okay. Take the time you need to find the answers that are right for you. You are your own person. And I hope you can see how amazing you are."

—SAMIRA AHMED, author of *Love, Hate & Other Filters*,
Internment and *Mad, Bad & Dangerous to Know*

"When I was ten years old, a man told me a sexual joke (it was about the way some women's bodies grow). I remember feeling scared right away—it was a mean joke and it made me uncomfortable that he wanted to talk to me this way. But what did I do? I laughed and pretended, for his sake, that I was unbothered. I couldn't imagine saying something as simple as 'that isn't funny to me,' or 'I don't want you to talk to me like that.' The instinct to accommodate other people is a powerful one. It took me a long time to become aware of it. What I wish I could say to my twelve-year-old (or even ten-year-old) self is: Rebecca, it is not your job to make other people comfortable while they are making you *uncomfortable*."

–REBECCA STEAD, author of *The List of Things That Will Not Change* and *When You Reach Me*

"What I wish twelve-year-old me had had the confidence to believe: If you say no, friends and boyfriends will still like you. And they'll have more respect for you. Being liked is nice, but being liked and respected is way better, so don't settle. You are worth more than that."

–DAPHNE BENEDIS-GRAB, author of *The Angel Tree* and *The Girl in the Wall*

"Dear 12-year-old Amy: Look—you've been called every name there is for a tomboy by now, and you know boys feel weird around you because you can play basketball, wire a light, and chop wood. What you don't know is that boys are about to test you. When they say something dirty, you don't have to out-do them to prove that you are cool. When they say something inappropriate, you don't have to keep it a secret because they won't talk to you anymore. When they reach out and grab you, you do not have to roll with that because you're one of the guys. You aren't one of the guys. You're you and you deserve respect."

–A.S. KING, author of *Dig* and *The Year We Fell From Space*

"A message to my self-conscious, small-town 12 year old self: Your crushes on boys may feel frustrating at first, until you realize it's because you're not attracted to them like a girl but as a boyish non-binary kid yourself. Maybe it's not fair that things will be more complicated for you than for your straight, cisgender classmates, but once you discover who you are, it'll feel like stepping out into the light after hiding someplace dark. You already know that you're a part of the LGBTQIA community, but what might surprise you is how long it'll take to pinpoint which letter (or several) best fits your attractions and identity. You are not falling behind your classmates; the process of discovering why you like who you like will just simply take a couple extra steps. While you may encounter some bumps along the way, be proud and stand tall. This is a journey you'll some-day be grateful for, that'll make you strong."

-A. J. SASS, author of *Ana on the Edge*

"You have good friends but boys don't seem to like you—except one boy who tried to make you do something you didn't want. I'm glad you said no (which isn't easy), and glad that, ultimately, you care a lot more about your friendships than crushes. I'm even glad boys don't like you! You won't be ready to think about doing anything more than kissing a boy—not for a long time, even until you're in college, when you'll feel like you're "behind" everyone where sex is concerned. But you're not. Not when you're twelve, or sixteen, or twenty. You're going to be figuring out who you are and what you want for many years to come . . . and the truth is that sometimes you would rather think about girls than boys. Take your time. Life is long. You don't have to know what you want right now."

-MARIE RUTKOSKI, author of *The Winner's Trilogy* and *The Midnight Lie*

"Hey there, Cindy Lou. I know it's tough being the second tallest girl in your grade and even more awkward because a lot of boys are eye level with your chest. It's not fair that more than one of your class-mates' moms commented on the fact that your body changed a little early, and that they think that means something about the kind of girl you might be. You were not put on this earth to make other people's parents comfortable with the fact that their kids are growing up. And by the way, love and romance and sexy fun time aren't about being a 'good girl' or 'bad girl.' They're about making the happiest, most satisfying choices for yourself when the time is right. For now, you're more than okay just as you are. Own your awesomeness!"

–CYNTHIA LEITICH SMITH, author of *Hearts Unbroken* and *Rain is Not My Indian Name*

FURTHER READING

Here is a list of Suggested Middle Grade and YA Novels* (Fun Reading, People!) for Further Pondering, Big Questioning, Little Questioning, Daydreaming, Fantasizing, and Everything in Between about Sex, Consent, Gender, Feminism, Sexual Identity, Romance, Love, and Just Being Who We Are, i.e. Human:

The Poet X by Elizabeth Acevedo
The Wrath & the Dawn by Renée Ahdieh
Simon Vs. The Homo Sapiens Agenda by Becky Albertalli
Saints and Misfits and *Love from A to Z* by S. K. Ali
What If It's Us by Becky Albertalli and Adam Silvera
Speak by Laurie Halse Anderson
Ivy Aberdeen's Letter to the World and *The Mighty Heart of Sunny St. James* by Ashley Herring Blake
Elatsoe by Darcie Little Badger
All-American Girl and *Ready or Not* by Meg Cabot
Graceling by Kristin Cashore
Little & Lion by Brandy Colbert
The Miseducation of Cameron Post by Emily M. Danforth
Just Listen, The Truth About Forever (and really all books) by Sarah Dessen
Pet by Akwaeke Emezi
Does My Head Look Big in This by Randa Abdel-Fattah

Give Me Some Truth by Eric Gansworth

George by Alex Gino

Forever For a Year, The Nerdy and the Dirty, and *The Handsome Girl & Her Beautiful Boy* by B. T. Gottfred

The Summer I Turned Pretty and To All the Boys I've Loved Before novels by Jenny Han

Intentions by Deborah Heiligman

Born Confused by Tanuja Desai Hidier

Me and Marvin Gardens by Amy Sarig King

The Love and Lies of Rukhsana Ali by Sabina Khan

Darius the Great is Not Okay by Adib Khorram

The Gospel of Winter, The Last True Love Story, and *Tradition* by Brendan Kiely

We Are Okay by Nina LaCour

The Left Hand of Darkness by Ursula K. Le Guin

Boy Meets Boy, Two Boys Kissing, and *Everyday* by David Levithan

Ash by Malinda Lo

The Disreputable History of Frankie Landau-Banks and all the *Ruby Oliver* books all by E. Lockhart

Amy & Roger's Epic Detour (and others) by Morgan Matson

Hurricane Season and *In the Role of Brie Hutchens* by Nicole Melleby

Only Ever Yours by Louise O'Neill

You Bring the Distant Near by Mitali Perkins

Luna by Julie Anne Peters

Opposite of Always by Justin A. Reynolds

Eleanor & Park by Rainbow Rowell

Bone Gap by Laura Ruby

If I Was Your Girl by Meredith Russo

Aristotle and Dante Discover the Secrets of the Universe by Benjamin Alire Sáenz

The Darkness Outside Us by Eliot Schrefer

The Moon Within by Aida Salazar

More Happy Than Not, They Both Die at the End (and others) by Adam Silvera

Odd One Out by Nic Stone

Marcelo in the Real Word by Francisco X. Stork

Blankets by Craig Thompson

Not that Kind of Girl, The List, and *We Are the Wildcats* by Siobhan Vivian

American Born Chinese by Gene Luen Yang

The Sun is Also a Star by Nicola Yoon

Frankly in Love by David Yoon

* Please note: There are SO MANY amazing stories I could have suggested, but these are just some of my favorites (in no particular order or grouping—just alphabetical). I considered suggesting some nonfiction readings and even some philosophy, but landed on just novels for now, because I think it's often through stories that we do some of our absolute best Big Questioning. Some of these novels are hilarious, some are sad, some will make you mad, some will make you SWOON (!!), some will make you long to be loved and romanced. All of them will help you to think (and you know how much I love thinking!) But it's an incomplete list—totally and absolutely incomplete! You should ask your friends and family and partners and teachers and mentors for other suggestions, too. But I promise you won't be sorry for reading any of these.

BIBLIOGRAPHY

Below is just a short (very short!) list of nonfiction books that are either referenced in this book, or are directly related to the Big Questions addressed in these pages. Just think of it as a *start* for some further reading, when you're ready!

Nonfiction Books about Children, Young Adults, College Students, Sex & Consent

Chimamanda Ngozi Adichie, *We Should All Be Feminists*, (New York, Anchor Books, 2015).

Elizabeth A. Armstrong and Laura T. Hamilton, *Paying for the Party: How College Maintains Inequality* (New York: Harvard University Press, 2015).

Lyn Mykel Brown and Carol Gilligan, *Meeting at the Crossroads: Women's Psychology and Girls' Development* (New York: Ballantine Books, 1993).

Laura M. Carpenter, *Virginity Lost: An Intimate Portrait of First Sexual Experiences* (New York University Press, 2005).

Jaquira Díaz *Ordinary Girls: A Memoir* (New York: Algonquin, 2019).

Eve Ensler, *The Apology* (New York: Bloomsbury, 2019).

Ronan Farrow, *Catch and Kill: Lies, Spies, and a Conspiracy to Protect Predators* (New York: Little, Brown, 2019).

Jennifer Finney Boylan, *She's Not There: A Life in Two Genders* (New York: Broadway Books, 2013).

Donna Freitas, *Consent: A Memoir of Unwanted Attention* (New York: Little, Brown, 2019).

Donna Freitas, *Consent on Campus: A Manifesto* (New York: Oxford University Press, 2018).

Donna Freitas, *Sex and the Soul, Updated Edition: Juggling Sexuality, Spirituality, Romance and Religion on America's College Campuses* (New York: Oxford University Press, 2015).

Christine J. Gardner, *Making Chastity Sexy: The Rhetoric of Evangelical Abstinence Campaigns* (Berkeley, CA: University of California Press, 2011).

Roxane Gay (Ed.), *Not That Bad, Dispatches from Rape Culture* (New York: Harper Perennial, 2018).

Patricia Hill Collins, *Black Feminist Thought: Knowledge, Consciousness, and the Politics of Empowerment* (London: Routledge, 2008).

Patricia Hill Collins, *Intersectionality as Critical Social Theory* (Durham, NC: Duke University Press, 2019).

Jennifer S. Hirsch and Shamus Khan, *Sexual Citizens: A Landmark Study of Sex, Power, and Assault on Campus* (New York: W.W. Norton, 2020).

Saeed Jones, *How We Fight for Our Lives: A Memoir* (New York: Simon & Schuster, 2019)

Jodi Kantor and Megan Twohey, *She Said: Breaking the Sexual Harassment Story That Helped Ignite a Movement* (New York: Penguin, 2019).

Jason King, *Faith with Benefits: Hookup Culture on Catholic Campuses* (New York: Oxford University Press, 2017).

Susan Kuklin, *Beyond Magenta: Transgender Teens Speak Out* (Somerville, MA: Candlewick, 2015).

Sharon Lamb, Lyn Mykel Brown, and Mark Tappan, *Packaging Boyhood: Saving Our Sons from Superheroes, Slackers, and Other Media Stereotypes* (New York: St. Martin's Press, 2009).

Sharon Lamb and Lyn Mykel Brown, *Packaging Girlhood: Rescuing Our Daughters from Marketers' Schemes* (New York: St. Martin's Griffin, 2007).

Chanel Miller, *Know My Name* (New York, Viking, 2019).

Shabana Mir, *Muslim American Women on Campus: Undergraduate Social Life and Identity* (Chapel Hill, North Carolina: University of North Carolina Press, 2016).

Sara Moslener, *Virgin Nation: Sexual Purity and American Adolescence* (New York: Oxford University Press, 2015).

Peggy Orenstein, *Boys & Sex: Young Men on Hookups, Love, Porn, Consent, and Navigation the New Masculinity* (New York: Harper, 2020).

Peggy Orenstein, *Girls & Sex: Navigating the Complicated New Landscape* (New York: Harper, 2017).

Kate Ott, *Sex + Faith: Talking to Your Children from Birth to Adolescence* (Louisville, KY: Westminster John Knox Press, 2013).

Alice Sebold, *Lucky* (New York: Scribner, 2017).

Rebecca Solnit, *Men Explain Things to Me* (Chicago: Haymarket Books, 2015).

Susan Stryker, *Transgender History: The Roots of Today's Revolution* (New York: Seal Press, 2017).

Deborah L. Tolman, *Dilemmas of Desire: Teenage Girls Talk About Sexuality* (New York: Harvard University Press, 2005).

Rebecca Traister, *Good and Mad: The Revolutionary Power of Women's Anger* (New York: Simon & Schuster, 2019).

Jessica Valenti, *Sex Object* (New York: Dey Street Books, 2017).

Lisa Wade, *American Hookup: The New Culture of Sex on Campus* (New York: W.W. Norton, 2018).

ACKNOWLEDGMENTS

This book would not exist without the amazing college students who have opened their hearts and minds to my questions over the last fifteen years. A big thanks to all of you for being in such open conversation with me.

I would like to thank all of my readers of drafts of this book, especially Eliot Schrefer, Robin Gow, and Nicole Melleby, as well as all of the Middle Grade and YA authors who took the time to speak advice to their twelve-year-old selves. I would also like to thank Adam Gidwitz and the organizers of SPA NYC, because it was during conversations at SPA that some fellow authors first planted the idea in my head that maybe I needed to write a kids book about sex and consent. Thank you to my amazing agent, Miriam Altshuler, my ever encouraging and endlessly patient editor, Nick Thomas, and to everyone at Levine Querido for taking a chance on this book and for letting me be the philosopher that I am! (That's you too, Arthur!) Thank you to my friends, colleagues, and husband, for being the conversation partners I need for all things related to my own Big Questioning. What in the world would I do without all of you?

ABOUT THE AUTHOR

DONNA FREITAS is a college professor whose research has focused on issues related to sex, romance, relationships, and consent for over a decade. She speaks about this work at schools across the country as well as on National Public Radio, *Today*, and many other radio and TV shows. Her books based on this research include *Sex and the Soul: Juggling Sexuality, Spirituality, Romance, and Religion*; *Consent on Campus: A Manifesto*; and *Consent: A Memoir of Unwanted Attention*, among others. Donna is also a long-time writer of YA and Middle Grade novels, including *The Possibilities of Sainthood* and *Gold Medal Summer*. She lives in Brooklyn, New York.

SOME NOTES ON THIS BOOK'S PRODUCTION

The art for the jacket was first begun as a pencil sketch, then finished digitally in Adobe Illustrator by Rodrigo Corral Studio. The text was set by Westchester Publishing Services in Danbury, CT in ITC Legacy Serif, a hand-drawn revival of Nicolas Jensen's 15th century types, designed by Ronald Arnholm in 1993. The display was set in The Hand, a handwritten font designed by Fanny Coulez and Julien Saurin for S&C Type, and Festivo LC, a textured and shadowed font designed by Ahmet Altun. The book was printed on 100gsm woodfree FSC™-certified paper and bound in Hong Kong.

Production was supervised by Leslie Cohen and Freesia Blizard
Book jacket designed by Rodrigo Corral Studio
Book interiors designed by Suet Y. Chong
Edited by Nick Thomas